Implementing Change

© Copyright R.E. Rokosz 2019

Published by Glorybound Publishing, Camp Verde, AZ

SAN 256-4564

10 9 8 7 6 5 4 3 2 1

Printed in the United States of America

ISBN 9781086874600

Library of Congress Cataloging-in-Publication data is available on file.

Rokosz, R.E., 1946-
        Implementing Change
1. Business   I. Title

www.gloryboundpublishing.com

www.amazon.com

Implementing Change:

The Dynamics of the Change Process

by
R. E. Rokosz

Glorybound Publishing
Camp Verde, Arizona USA
in the year 2019

Author's Note

While the information presented here is dated, it is none the less still applicable in today's business environment.

It should also be note that while aerospace was the industry selected for this study, the end result of this work indicates that information presented here is pertaining to successfully implementing change is applicable to any industry, organization, or association.

The bottom-line is that the findings indicate there is nothing unique about implementing change.

Appreciation and Dedication

Appreciation

Appreciation and thanks go out to two fine Martin Marietta Human Resources and Development specialists. These gentlemen provided an enormous amount of materials support in the development of this for the work. Without them this product would lessor in content and quality.

Dedication

This work is dedicated to my wonderful cohorts without whom the workplace would have been quite dull and boring and most importantly to my wife Darlene for her tireless support in holding down the fort and managing the family through the two years it took me to complete my degree.

IMPLEMENTING CHANGE :The Dynamics of the Change Process

A Project

by

Richard E. Rokosz

September, 1991

Running Head: IMPLEMENTING CHANGE

Submitted to the MSM Program of Regis College in partial fulfillment of the requirements for the degree of Master of Science in Management

Table of Contents

LIST OF FIGURES

LIST OF APPENDICES

Appendix   Title

Abstract

Corporations are continuously striving to improve their products and services by frequently introducing changes within their organizations. These changes seldom achieve the intended goals, are short-lived, and are soon replaced by other improvement initiatives.

Research, including interviews, observations, surveys, and documents written on the subject of change, indicates six Key Success Factors are vital to successfully implementing change. They include:

1. senior management's initiation and active participation in the change,

2. the development of a structured implementation plan,

3. clear communications with all levels of the organization,

4. training of the participants,

5. measuring performance, and

6. a reward and recognition program.

The probability of success is significantly higher when all six factors are present. Omission or lack of proper consideration of any one factor can increase the risk of failure.

The Key Success Factors reside within three families of factors:

1. the workforce,

2. management, and

3. the organization.

These factors, along with the underlying conditions of politics, technology, culture, and risk, form a comprehensive profile of the factors involved in a successful implementation.

The author has created a model which addresses the various change factors, an action sequence figure depicting the six Key Success Factors, and an Implementation Checklist to serve as tools in assisting managers desiring to successfully implement change in their organizations.

INTRODUCTION

Attempts at making organizations more productive are virtually as old as time. In 2000 B.C., Egyptian leaders used an instruction book which told them how to communicate with subordinates. Moses used a span of control of one foreman for every ten workers in preparing for the exodus from Egypt. Since these earliest of times experts in the field of management profess to have the answers for improving productivity. They propose changes they believe will solve the problems they currently face. McGill (1988) states that quite often, the solutions do not consider the complexity of the situation and prove to be only a quick fix. We now live in a society that demands instant satisfaction. Our culture is one that tends to say that if problems can be presented and solved in thirty minutes on a television sitcom, then we should be able to resolve issues in the workplace just as quickly. Managers in industry know they will receive recognition and status based upon achievement. Observations have shown that frequently they look for a quick way to solve the problem so they can move to the next task. Recognizing that time is of the essence, they are drawn to actions which offer simple solutions.

Quick fixes have a significant impact on the business and the workforce. A tremendous amount of time, energy, and capital are invested in these endeavors. Frequently, changes over a short period of time, often overlap, cause confusion, and lower the morale of an already highly stressed workforce. This is the environment in which business operates today. What can be done to bring about orderly lasting changes that will benefit society, the corporation, and its workforce?

This paper looks at the various factors involved in implementing change within the aerospace industry. The effect each factor has upon a successful implementation is presented and discussed. Research in the form of managerial interviews, personal observations/participation, reviews of previous aerospace employee surveys, and a literature search was done as part of this paper.

An aerospace industry survey was specifically designed and conducted as part of this project. The objective of the survey was to determine if certain factors influenced the attempt to implement a change in either a positive or negative way. The survey results substantiated the research and supported the information found in documents published on the subject of change. As a result of the infor mation gathered from the sources identified above, several Key Success Factors emerged. They are discussed in detail in the following sections of this paper. An implementation checklist was developed and incorporated into this thesis as a guide in helping managers successfully implement change.

Several changes researched in this study appear in Appendix A. A list of them and the most common reasons for their limited success are identified.

RESEARCH METHODOLOGY

This study used five methods to gather, assess, and evaluate data. These methods were personal observations/participation, management interviews, a review of multiple company survey data, a literature review, and a survey of several major aerospace companies.

Personal Observation/Participation

As a central manager not assigned to a specific program, I was able to observe several changes which attempted to improve productivity and/or reduce costs within our company. This position allowed me neutrality in witnessing and documenting the events as they occurred. This position also allowed me to observe one particular change as it was being implemented across four different programs. I was able to monitor this change and view the different approaches used by program managers during its implementation.

The opportunity to observe changes being implemented provided a significant amount of information which I considered when I participated in the implementation of several changes. These changes are discussed in the Application of Findings section of this paper.

Management Interviews

I interviewed two groups of managers at Lockheed Martin *(formerly Martin Marietta)* for this project. The interviews were conducted by telephone and in person. The first group consisted of eight directors from technical and business development organizations who are members of the company president's staff. These senior executives average thirty-eight years of aerospace experience. They have been in program management positions and participated in significant productivity orientated changes in aerospace throughout their careers.

The second group consisted of twelve engineers who have managed or are currently managing programs. This group averages twenty-six years of experience in the aerospace industry, and have held positions of increasing responsibility on several programs.

These individuals were asked to identify from their past experiences; those factors they found had either a favorable or unfavorable effect on their attempt to implement a change.

It should be noted that several other individuals, including a group of eleven Martin Marietta company employees participating in a class on managing change, were directly involved in this study. The group consisting of representatives from various levels of the workforce, provided information which helped verify my research.

Company Surveys

Three employee surveys conducted by Martin Marietta were reviewed. The first was a departmental study of 120 administrative support personnel held in March of 1987. The objective of this study was to assess departmental performance. The second was a companywide survey administered in June of 1988, to over 4000 employees at all levels and across all organizational departments. This survey was designed to obtain the employees' general impressions of company operations. The third survey was designed to assess the impact of a product improvement initiative and was conducted among 150 engineers working on significant programs in August of 1989. These three surveys provided background information which helped identify factors which affect implementing a change.

Literature Search

Many documents have been published on the subject of change. Texts on organizational behavior, communications, managing corporate change, planning, leadership, team building, and new paradigm management were reviewed. Each of these works was in itself a comprehensive document; however, by combining them with the data gathered from the other research methods, I generated a list of factors which have an impact upon implementing a change. These factors were then tested in an aerospace industry survey.

Aerospace Industry Survey

I surveyed 20 major aerospace companies in September of 1990. The companies were asked to complete a questionnaire which identified how successful they were in implementing changes within their organizations. The survey identified three categories: 1) highly successful, 2) somewhat successful, and 3) unsuccessful changes. The criteria used in determining success are displayed in figure 1.

CATEGORY	CRITERIA
HIGHLY SUCCESSFUL	ACHIEVED SIGNIFICANT GAINS USED FOR A SIGNIFICANT PERIOD OF TIME ACCEPTED BY THE WORKFORCE
SOMEWHAT SUCCESSFUL	ACHIEVED EXPECTED GAINS MODERATE USE OVER TIME WORKFORCE WAS NEUTRAL
UNSUCCESSFUL	ACHIEVED LITTLE OR NO GAIN MINIMAL OR NO UTILIZATION WORKFORCE WAS NEGATIVE

Figure 1 Survey Categories

A generic set of questions was developed and used for all three categories. A copy of the survey is included as Appendix B. The companies were also asked to indicate whether their organizations were matrix or non-matrix structured. The objective of this question was to determine if one type of organizational structure was more conducive to implementing change than another. The survey results are summarized and documented in Appendix C. The somewhat successful responses were combined with the successful responses since they were virtually identical.

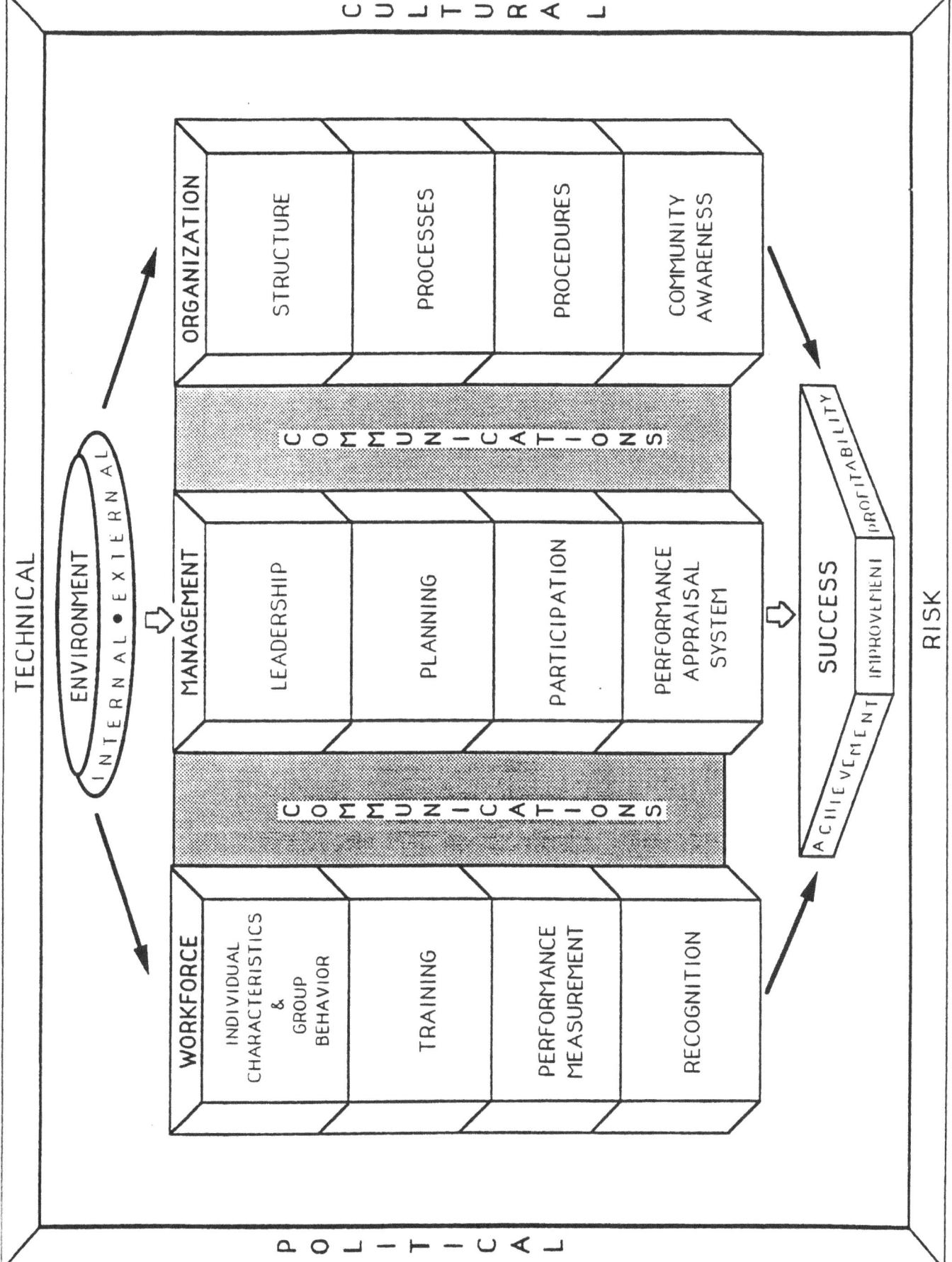

Figure 2

Analysis of the data generated by the aerospace survey as well as other research indicated that many factors come into play when an attempt is made to implement a change. I have constructed a change model (figure 2 on page 15), which identifies these factors and their relationships. The book "Organizational Behavior and Performance" by Szilagyi, & Wallace (1990) provided material which served as the basis from which this model was developed.

FAMILY OF FACTORS

The factors influencing change tended to fall within specific natural groupings. I have identified these groupings as families: the workforce family, the management family, and the organization family. These three units form the core element of a change and are the focus of my change model. They are interrelated and continuously interacting with each other.

KEY SUCCESS FACTORS

There resides within the families a set of six common factors. The literature researched consistently contained these factors. Since the rate of success increased significantly when all six were present, I have identified them as key success factors. These key success factors are:

1) senior management initiation and active participation

2) a structured action plan

3) clear communication of goals and objectives

4) training the participants

5) measurement of the process

6) a reward and recognition program.

All but one of these Key Success Factors is contained within one of the three families. The sixth factor, communications, serves to link all the other factors together. **The key success factors will be discussed within the Family of Factor structure**.

I have aligned the key success factors in an action sequence diagram shown in figure 3. This figure represents the activities that should occur in a specific sequence to effect a successful change.

Figure 3

UNDERLYING FACTORS

I have also established a set of secondary factors identified as **underlying conditions**. They are environmental, technical, political, and cultural forces and the element of risk. These underlying factors also influence change and are discussed in a subsequent section of this paper.

Workforce Family of Factors

The mainstay of any organization and in many cases, its most valuable resource is the workforce. This element is mainly responsible for carrying out management's objectives and implementing changes. Workers are most comfortable when they know what is to be accomplished and are provided with proven techniques to perform their assigned tasks. Getting them to change requires management's recognition of the following characteristics.

Individual and Group Performance. Recognition of the employee as an individual is of prime importance. A person has specific personal goals and objectives. Efforts must be made to understand their needs and channel them to align with those of the corporation. Use of alignment techniques as described in Kiefer & Stroh (1984) or Ishikawa's (1987) Master Vector Concept are excellent tools to help accomplish this objective. The alignment of personal and company objectives will facilitate a cooperative working relationship between management and the employee and will result in a real productivity gain. Communication of the objective and feedback of performance are essential. Bolman (1989) states, "workers are likely to be more committed to their work and less alienated when they understand how it fits into a coherent whole" (p. 246).

Group dynamics of work teams play a significant role in implementing change. The interdependency of people within a group as well as the group's interactions with other groups must be understood to have effective processes in the workplace. Belgard, Fisher, Rayner (1988) indicate that careful consideration must be given when selecting team members to ensure that they possess the appropriate skills and characteristics needed to work within a group. Training and education of the workforce in utilizing group operating techniques is beneficial and in many cases, necessary. Whenever changes in product quality, quantity, or processes are required, training must be provided to inform and educate all levels of the workforce.

Training. **(KEY FACTOR)** This factor surfaced in every company survey, several interviews, and many published texts. It is that which is most asked for by the workforce and least provided by management. Oliver White (1981) describes job education as "usually underestimated, under budgeted, and not understood" (p. 370). Much has been written recently regarding the lack of training or orientation being given to the American workforce. A Business Week article (October 8, 1990) states that the Japanese auto worker receives 370 hours of training compared to just 46 hours for their American counterparts. Quite often, the reason given is that the project is behind schedule, so there is no time to properly train the employee. The result is a product whose design and manufacture reflect the efforts that have gone into training the workforce to produce it. Without proper training, performance measurements are not as effective as they could be.

Performance Measurement. **(KEY FACTOR)** The importance of performance measurements was identified in several texts and the Martin Marietta Productivity Improvement (PI) survey. The workforce recognized the importance of this factor. Their responses to the PI survey indicated a willingness to have their performance measured and a strong desire to participate in developing the measurements. Quality gurus such as Deming (1982), Juran (1989), and Crosby (1979) all speak out on the importance of measuring performance. They argue that quality cannot be controlled, and improvements cannot be made unless the process is understood by those tasked to perform the work. The National Baldridge Award also recognizes the importance of measurements. Questions in five of their seven categories assessing quality pertain to performance measurements. Measurements play a vital part in understanding any process. Appropriate and meaningful measurements should be taken, and the data analyzed before any action is taken to correct or improve a process. This point is graphically illustrated in the section of this paper, which discusses the implementation of concurrent engineering.

<u>Recognition</u>. **(KEY FACTOR)** Interviews with senior managers indicated they were aware of the value in recognizing employee job performance. The opinion that "just having a job is adequate recognition," is not acceptable to today's workforce. The aerospace industry survey data indicated that the workforce felt a real need to be recognized for their performance. A specific reward program was installed in 57% of the successful initiatives, whereas only 11% of the unsuccessful attempts indicated doing so. Recognition should not be limited to financial remuneration. The awarding of pins, patches, plaques, and the like also serves to recognize the employee's contribution to a successful implementation of a change.

It should be noted here that recognition of team performance is also significant. Managers are now more often turning to the team approach to get the job done. Continued success and perpetuation of team activities rely on recognition. Once again, the aerospace survey dramatically points this out. No team rewards were established in the unsuccessful attempts, versus 87% of the successful attempts which recognized both individual and team contributions. A technical director who successfully implemented a change stated that his teams asked for better tools and simplified procedures as their form of compensation. This data substantiates the fact that people will do good work when given clear direction, proper training, appropriate measurements, and rewards for performance.

MANAGEMENT Family of Factors

Research shows that successful changes are most often introduced by the senior levels of management, namely the CEO, company president, vice-presidents, or directors. As leaders, they recognize that well-orchestrated changes will increase productivity. Several books on leadership also indicate that change must be introduced from the top management because the majority of organizations are highly mechanistic. They are structured in a hierarchy that encourages employees to perform work in a standardized manner. This structure discourages creativity in workers and relies on senior management to provide new direction.

Leadership. (**KEY FACTOR**) Bennis (1989) defines the difference between leaders and managers as "leaders are people who do the right thing; managers are people who do things right" (p. 18). Tichy (1986) further describes managers as individuals who maintain the balance of operations in an organization. They identify with the organization and seek solutions within the framework of the existing structure. Leaders, on the other hand, are individuals who create new approaches and find new areas to explore. They are more intuitive and accept risk where opportunities and rewards are high. They possess the ability to excite people about their ideas and get them to participate in the activity. The struggle occurred within an organization when managers dedicated to maintaining the status quo encounter leaders committed to changing it. Successful change requires leaders to assess a situation, develop a plan, determine the risk, and communicate with others in a way that will gain their support and acceptance. Successful leadership today goes beyond just giving directions. It requires dealing with the workforce in a charismatic, participative manner. The importance of management participation will be addressed in the following section.

Planning. (**KEY FACTOR**) Recall Lewis Carroll's story of *Alice in Wonderland*. Alice asked the Cheshire Cat which road she should take, to which the cat replied that it depends on where you want to go. Alice responded she don't much care, to which the cat answered than any road would do.   Such lack of direction, or not knowing where one wants to go, can have a significant impact on the success of the proposed change. Results of the aerospace survey dramatically indicate the importance of goal-oriented planning. The rate of success for those changes that established detailed plans was 87%, whereas only 50% of the unsuccessful changes had established detail plans. The on-time completion rate doubled when plans were developed, versus where they were not. Once the change had been planned, the survey indicated senior management actively participated in successful implementations.

An implementation checklist has been created and is discussed in the Risk section. It addresses all of the factors identified in this paper and should be used as a tool when planning a change.

Participation. **(KEY FACTOR)** Two cases are cited from personal observation in which the involvement of senior management made a significant difference between success and failure. In the successful implementation, the technical director played an active role in promoting and implementing the change. He communicated the plan at special staff meetings to everyone in the organization. He was present and actively participated in small working sessions held at all levels of the organization. The workforce observing his involvement realized the importance of the change. Their support of the change was directly proportional to the level of visibility and participation by the director.

The second case involved the same initiative but achieved different results. In this situation, the director, although in favor of the change, did very little. He identified the desired change to his organization as something **they** should do. He communicated the information only to his staff level managers. No one below the staff level was informed. No detailed plan was established, nor was any orientation or training provided to the group responsible for implementation. Consequently, very little progress was made in improving the operations of this project. Measurement data was late in coming and did not provide evidence of any significant improvement.

Performance Appraisal System. The importance of a reward system has been previously discussed. The success of any change also requires the establishment of a system that recognizes the contributions of both individuals and groups. The responsibility to establish and monitor this system rests with management. Several different methods exist. They vary from Herzberg's KITA (kick in the pants) approach to current programs described by Bolman (1989), which focus on job enrichment. It is essential to recognize that holding people accountable for their work is critical to success. It is just as important to realize that people will be more productive when their work is challenging and stimulating. Most people want to know how well they are performing. They should be told promptly whether their performance is in line with management's expectations. The appraisal system should take all of these things into consideration in addressing the employee's performance in support of the organization's goals and objectives.

ORGANIZATION Family of Factors

Organizations are the manifestation of company management and its mission. The organizational structure should be a direct reflection of the company's desired goals and objectives.

Structure.   Hambrick and Finkelstein (1987) wrote that larger more mature organizations have developed a consistent set of responses, standard operating procedures, and habits that have been reinforced by success in their environment. Growth and diversification alter a company's structure and impacts its ability to change. An organization's structure provides the shell or framework within which the desired work is accomplished. It supports the corporate culture and quite often reinforces its authority. Bolman (1989) states, "many organizational problems are caused by structure more than by people" (p. 53). The mechanistic structure found in most organizations today emphasizes specialization, compartmentalization of work, detail roles and responsibilities, and top-down control. This structure leads to the establishment of walls and roadblocks within an organization. The way these barriers can be overcome is by having less structure. Bennis (1989) expresses it in the following statement "With less structure and more leadership, American business might begin to recover its verve, energy, and spunk" (p. 80).

Processes. Processes are the methods by which work is accomplished. For productivity gains to be realized, we must change the way we do work, that modifies our processes. Morhman (1989) states, "If an organization truly wants to change the way it manages, it may need to change all or most of its major systems " (p. 261). Changing a single system may be more disruptive than constructive since one system is usually interwoven with others.

Mohrman says few organizations have ever simultaneously changed several systems within their operations. Most are unwilling to try this unless they are facing a crisis. Personal observations of attempts at process improvement indicate that the majority of our workforce has minimal knowledge of any given company system. In addition to a lack of understanding company operations, attempts to change are met with resistance due to lack of ownership of the process, lack of understanding the proposed change, and or fear that the change would negatively impact the organization such as a reduction in staff. Employees are less likely to support a change if they do not understand it or know what impact it may have on them. Fear of the unknown is also very evident in the observations. A successful change implementation requires that these issues be addressed and overcome. It is also essential for the owner of the process to support the change and be willing to play an active role in its implementation.

Procedures. Whereas processes are the techniques for getting the work accomplished, procedures formalize the company operating methodology. They describe the activity and document the roles and responsibilities of the various departments. Procedures should be written to be flexible in documenting methods or techniques, yet allow work to be accomplished in ways that meet the needs of the program. Standardization should center around issues which involve human safety, the law, and compliance to government regulations and specifications. Attempts to legislate discipline into a system are rarely effective. People are more likely to adherence to procedures when they understand the requirement and the consequences should they fail to comply.

Community Awareness. This factor was not addressed in any of the material researched, but the emphasis being placed on it today warrant its discussion. Consideration must be given to situations in which a proposed change will have an impact on the community. The indirect or tertiary relationship between the corporation and the community is one that must be considered. Special interest groups can stop or prohibit a company from implementing a desired change. The need for corporations to plan and act responsibly has never been greater. Concerns about the environment have many people worried we are leaving a terrible mess for future generations. Corporate policy must address this issue. Companies provide funds to modify their processes in order to safeguard natural resources. The contention that funds are not available in operating budgets becomes a moot point when faced with a multimillion-dollar task to clean up a hazardous spill. Senior management should be willing to work with various federal, state, and local officials on any issue impacting the proposed change. The quality of life can be maintained when the appropriate resources, both private and corporate, are brought to bear cooperatively.

Communications **(KEY FACTOR)** Communications is depicted in the model as the link which allows the factors to interact with each other. The worker of today is much more inquisitive and demanding of information than in the past. Naisbitt in Megatrends 2000 (1990) states that we cannot expect an employee to function at his optimum unless management has successfully conveyed the big picture to him. This fact was collaborated by the responses given by employees in the Martin Marietta company surveys. Business managers in the 1990s must win employee loyalty, obtain their commitment, and earn their respect. Future success depends on how well management communicates its ideas, goals, and objectives to the workforce. Change will be successfully implemented when, as Tichy (1986) says, "Information about the environment ... should be widely disseminated through the organization so that all of the members understand the challenge" (p. 56). One of the reasons contributing to success is how well the message is conveyed. People will be more committed when they understand how all the pieces fit into the picture.

Underlying Factors

An organization can be viewed as a system that receives input, performs work, and generates an output. There are other factors which influence the performance of the system or attempts to change it. I have identified these factors as **underlying conditions.**

Environmental Condition. All companies operate within two environments, internal and external. The internal environment is comprised of elements such as the policies, procedures, the workforce, suppliers, customers, and competitors. These elements in and of themselves can and do influence business operations and can be the reason why change should occur.

The external elements include the economy, government policies, natural resources, and international activities. They are outside the scope of the company's normal internal operations and form a tertiary relationship with the organization. They represent indirect forces over which management has little or no control. These factors must be recognized and dealt with for the company to remain competitive.

Analysis of the data gathered from the surveys indicates that change is likely to occur as a result of events originating from within one or both of the above environments. Organizations can choose either to react to these forces or anticipate them. In any event, management quite often feels an over-powering need to change based upon what is transpiring in either the internal or external environment. Consideration must be given to ensure that the proposed change is warranted and not just a response to what is trendy or popular at the time.

Political Condition. The term political has several meanings. Its use here is not that of being manipulative for personal interest, but rather to represent the technique by which management obtains the resources required to perform the work from a limited base or pool. A manager's success is directly related to his ability to lend, borrow, exchange, and negotiate for limited resources. Success is predicated on knowing the limitations and being able to influence others to provide the resources necessary to accomplish the task. It should be recognized that power in the form of managerial authority is a driving force here. Effective use of power will quite often influence the outcome of an activity.

Technical Condition. A significant technical problem or new technological development can pose a serious threat to existing and future business. Management must recognize this and formulate a strategy whereby the appropriate organizational elements are brought together to address the situation. Failure to do so can have long term ramifications such as loss of technological advantage, market share, and possibly failure of the business. The ideal situation would have the business development strategist anticipating future needs and participating with the technical engineering managers in developing plans which will allow the company to be pro-active rather than reactive.

<u>Cultural Condition.</u> Organizations are held together by a set of shared beliefs. These beliefs are known as the company's culture. It reflects the values, norms, objectives, and expectations shared by those in the organization. The culture which resides within the organizational structure can be an excellent shield to hide behind when a change is proposed. It was not uncommon when observing attempts to implement change to hear the following: "We don't do that here", or "That won't work here because", or "We're different", or "We have never done it that way." The culture is formed or modified in response to the organization's mission. It reflects the drive and imagination of everyone involved in the activity. Culture begins to take shape when rules governing work, and a reward system are formally documented. This is when accepted behavior is defined, and attitudes essential for success are formulated. Research indicates that culture quite often is viewed as having a negative influence on attempts to change. It becomes the proverbial brick wall or the bureaucracy that stands in the way of progress. Overcoming this resistance requires a well thought out plan. The key to whether resistance forces deter the organization from making the needed change rests with management.

The metaphor of a rope is used by Tichy (1983) to describe the interactions of the technical, political, and cultural conditions and can be used here to underscore a couple of points. First, from a distance, the individual strands are indistinguishable. It is difficult to separate the working of the technical from the political and cultural elements. Second, should the rope become unraveled, the technical, political, and cultural strands can work at cross-purposes, thus weakening the organization. Management must be aware of their organizational fabric and work to keep it from becoming unraveled due to problems originating within these three conditions.

  Risk. Although the risk is inherent in many of the factors already discussed, it can also influence change. The success of any change requires an in-depth assessment of the situation. To help with this assessment several questions should be asked; such as why is the change necessary, what will it accomplish, who will be tasked to do it, or when should it be done? The list of questions to ask can be extensive. Careful consideration must be given to all the factors identified in the factors influencing change model with particular emphasis being placed on the Key Success Factors. These key success factors again are 1) senior management initiation and active participation, 2) a structured action plan, 3) clear communication of goals and objectives, 4) training of the participants, 5) measurement of the process, and 6) a reward and recognition program.

  Risk in implementing a change can be reduced by using the checklist found on pages 25, 26, and 26. The checklist was created using data gathered from the aerospace industry survey as well as various resource documents. It contains questions associated with each of the factors discussed in this paper. Screening a change through this checklist will increase the probability of success.

PAGE 1

IMPLEMENTATION QUESTIONNAIRE

QUESTIONS	YES/NO	ACTIONS TO ASSURE SUCCESS
KEY SUCCESS FACTORS		
MANAGEMENT		
DO YOU HAVE APPROPRIATE SENIOR MANAGEMENT APPROVAL?		
IS SR. MGMT. COMMITTED TO BE VISIBLE AND ACTIVELY PARTICIPATE?		
PLANNING		
HAS A STRUCTURED PLAN WHICH CONSIDERS ALL FACTORS BEEN DEVELOPED THAT INCLUDES SPECIFIC, ATTAINABLE, AND REALISTIC MILESTONES AND GOALS?		
HAS A REALISTIC SCHEDULE BEEN ESTABLISHED AND ACCEPTED BY THE PARTICIPANTS?		
COMMUNICATIONS		
HAVE YOU DEVELOPED A STRATEGY TO CLEARLY COMMUNICATE YOUR GOALS AND OBJECTIVES TO ALL LEVELS OF THE ORGANIZATION?		
HAVE TECHNIQUES FOR PROVIDING FEEDBACK BEEN DETERMINED?		
TRAINING		
HAS A TRAINING PLAN BEEN ESTABLISHED THAT WILL EDUCATE AND TRAIN ALL LEVELS OF THE ORGANIZATION?		
ARE THE APPROPRIATE RESOURCES AVAILABLE OR ATTAINABLE TO PROPERLY TRAIN THE PARTICIPANTS?		
MEASUREMENTS		
HAVE APPROPRIATE MEASUREMENTS BEEN DEVELOPED TO ASSESS PERFORMANCE TO STATED GOALS AND OBJECTIVES?		
ARE THEY CAPABLE OF BEING MODIFIED OR REPLACED WITH PROGRESS?		
REWARD AND RECOGNITION		
HAVE YOU ESTABLISHED A PROGRAM THAT WILL PROVIDE APPROPRIATE AND TIMELY RECOGNITION FOR THE PARTICIPANTS?		

IMPLEMENTATION QUESTIONNAIRE

QUESTIONS	YES/NO	ACTIONS TO ASSURE SUCCESS
WORK FORCE FACTORS		
INDIVIDUAL & GROUP CONSIDERATIONS		
HAS CONSIDERATION BEEN GIVEN FOR THE VALUES AND CONCERNS OF THE INDIVIDUAL WORKER?		
HAS CONSIDERATION BEEN TO GIVEN TO THE CHARACTERISTICS OF GROUP DYNAMICS?		
MANAGEMENT FACTORS		
LEADERSHIP		
IS SENIOR MANAGEMENT PREPARED TO MODIFY THEIR BEHAVIOR AND MANAGEMENT STYLE AS REQUIRED TO SUPPORT THIS INITIATIVE?		
ARE THEY WILLING TO SERVE AS MENTORS AND PROVIDE LEADERSHIP TO SUBORDINATES AS REQUIRED?		
ORGANIZATIONAL FACTORS		
STRUCTURE		
HAS CONSIDERATION BEEN GIVEN TO PREVIOUS ATTEMPTS TO CHANGE?		
WILL THE CURRENT STRUCTURE SUPPORT THE CHANGE PROCESS?		
PROCESS & PROCEDURES		
WILL CURRENT PROCESSES OR PROCEDURES HAVE TO BE MODIFIED?		
WILL ANY NEW ONES HAVE TO BE WRITTEN?		
COMMUNITY IMPACT		
WILL THIS CHANGE HAVE AN ADVERSE EFFECT ON THE LOCAL COMMUNITY?		
HAS THIS IMPACT BEEN ADDRESSED WITH THE APPROPRIATE CORPORATE AND COMMUNITY LEADERS?		

QUESTIONS	YES/NO	ACTIONS TO ASSURE SUCCESS
UNDERLYING CONSIDERATIONS		
ENVIRONMENT HAS DUE CONSIDERATION BEEN GIVEN TO THE VALIDITY AND SOURCE OF THIS PROPOSED CHANGE?		
IS IT REQUIRED OR BEING DONE IN RESPONSE TO A CURRENT TREND?		
TECHNICAL HAVE THE TECHNOLOGICAL IMPACTS BEEN GIVEN ADEQUATE CONSIDERATION?		
WILL THIS CHANGE GIVE US A PREEMPTIVE CAPABILITY?		
POLITICAL HAVE YOU NEGOTIATED FOR THE PROPER RESOURCES?		
HAS A PLAN BEEN DEVELOPED TO OBTAIN THOSE RESOURCES THAT ARE IN SHORT SUPPLY?		
CULTURAL IS THE PREVAILING CORPORATE CULTURE AMENABLE TO CHANGE?		
HAVE THE AREAS OF RESISTANCE BEEN IDENTIFIED?		
RISK ARE THE NECESSARY RESOURCES BOTH HUMAN AND CAPITAL AVAILABLE?		
HAVE YOU IDENTIFIED WHO IS ACCOUNTABLE FOR THE VARIOUS TASKS?		
HAVE YOU ADDRESSED ANY GAPS THE PLAN MAY CONTAIN?		
ARE THE RESPONSIBLE PARTIES PREPARED TO NEGOTIATE AND COMPROMISE TO ATTAIN THE OVERALL OBJECTIVE?		

APPLICATIONS OF THE FINDINGS

The factors impacting the success of a change identified in this paper have been used in several applications. They include the implementation of Concurrent Engineering, assisting in developing the Engineering Resource Planning process, as course material in an employee training program, and updating the company Annual Performance Improvement Program.

Concurrent Engineering The Key Success Factors were used in the implementation of a change known as Concurrent Engineering. Briefly, Concurrent Engineering is the process by which several departments simultaneously participate in the development of a product. This activity was begun two years ago at the direction of the Vice President of Technical Operations. He asked the technical directors of three programs to assess the way they were designing products. They were asked to modify their process to reduce errors and improve quality. The charts in figures 4, 5, 6, and 7 on page 34 show the reduction in errors in producing engineering after the change to Concurrent Engineering was introduced.

It should be noted that each project implemented this change by developing a plan, communicating the objective, having management play an active role, measuring performance, and rewarding the participants. The program focused on getting all the right people involved from the start of an activity, so they can all develop the product together. Communication was accomplished through large and small group staff meetings, company newsletters, and productivity improvement display boards. The technical directors provided hands-on leadership by way of active participation. Getting people to work together in groups on this project was very important. Recognizing the role group dynamics plays in improving productivity, the High-Performance Work Team (HPWT) approach was applied to this process. A three-day training program was developed and used to supplement and reinforce the interdepartmental activity. A special awards program was implemented to recognize individual and team performance. Pictures were taken of the participants and displayed with a summary of their accomplishment on specially installed productivity improvement status boards. These status boards were also used to show specific performance improvements, such as the data contained in figures 4, 5, 6, and 7. Data were displayed from all programs participating in the Concurrent Engineering initiative. This initiative has realized significant productivity gains and is being implemented on each new program.

Engineering Resource Planning (ERP) The purpose of this initiative is to define the tasks and processes the engineering organization will perform as part of a new manufacturing system being implemented in the corporation. The Key Success Factors were used in developing the section about engineering management. The factors were introduced as a list of actions senior management should address as part of their responsibilities in helping bring about mission success. An assessment team consisting of twenty mid-level managers considered these and many other factors. They identified five of the six Key Success Factors as top actions to be taken by management to ensure mission success.

Training Tool The factors influencing change model in figure 2 on page 15, along with the six Key Success Factors form part of the curriculum for a class I have developed. The course, now being taught at Martin Marietta, is entitled "Managing Change" and addresses issues related to successfully implementing a change within an aerospace company.

Annual Performance Improvement Program (APIP) Martin Marietta, on a yearly basis, looks at the various measurements to determine performance. The 1991 APIP planning process used the Key Success Factors as a guide in helping evolve the measurements for the new year. They are also being considered as a tool to help inform employees and gain their support of the 1991 plan.

Future Application The individuals who will benefit the most from this research are future program managers. Martin Marietta provides training in all aspects of program management for these people. I will propose to the Technology Training Organization the addition of a module to their current training program which emphasizes the Key Success Factors action sequence model and the implementation checklist as tools that can help successfully implement change.

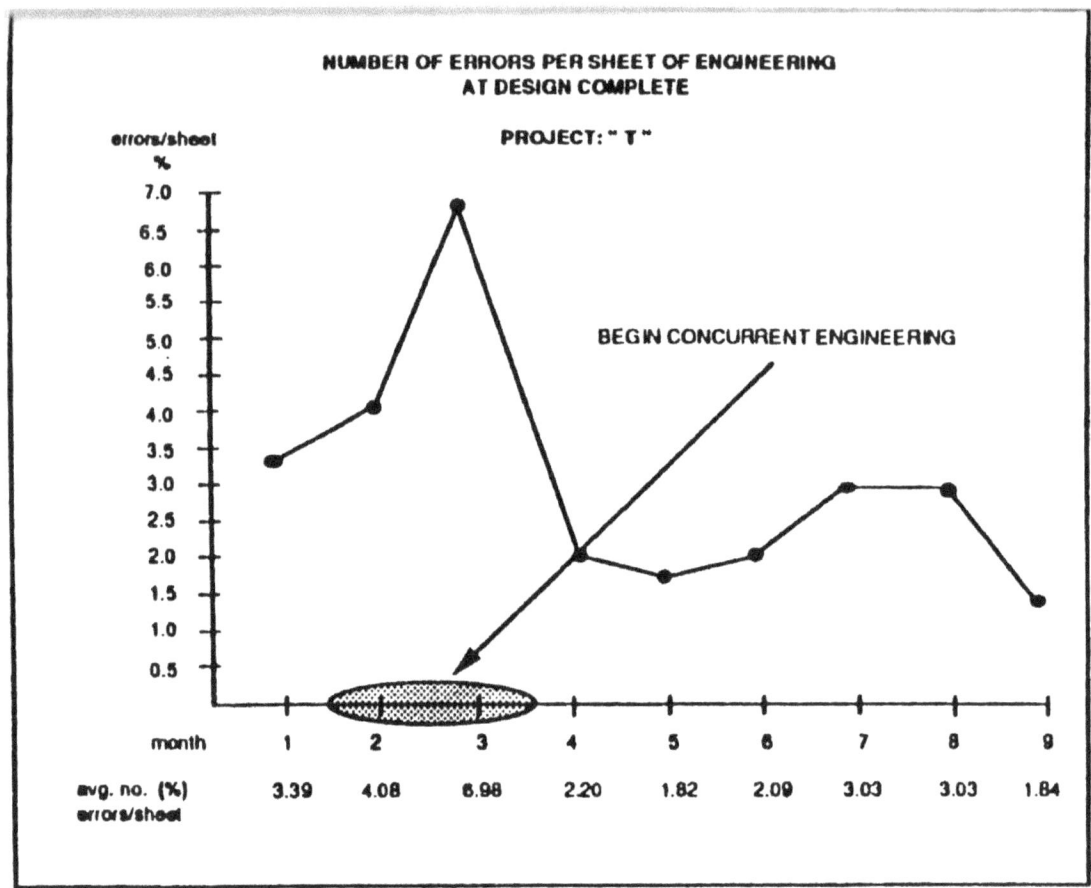

Figure 4

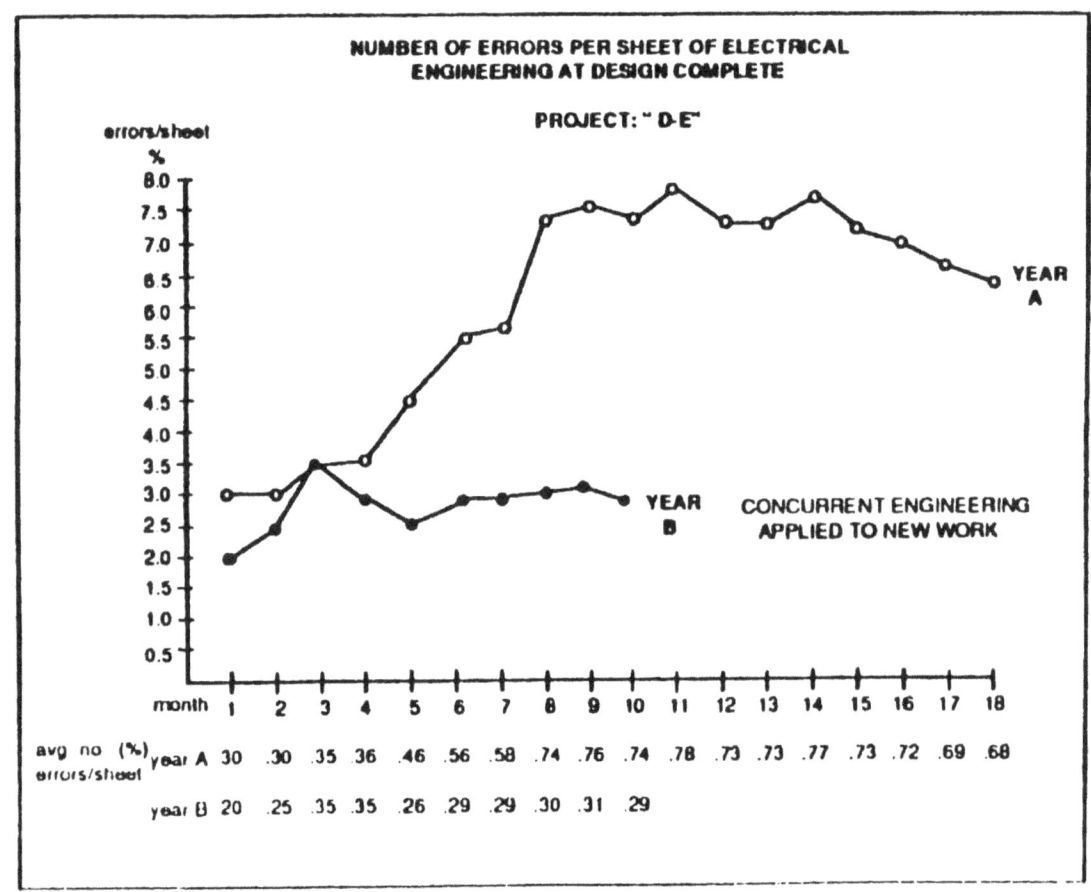

Figure 6

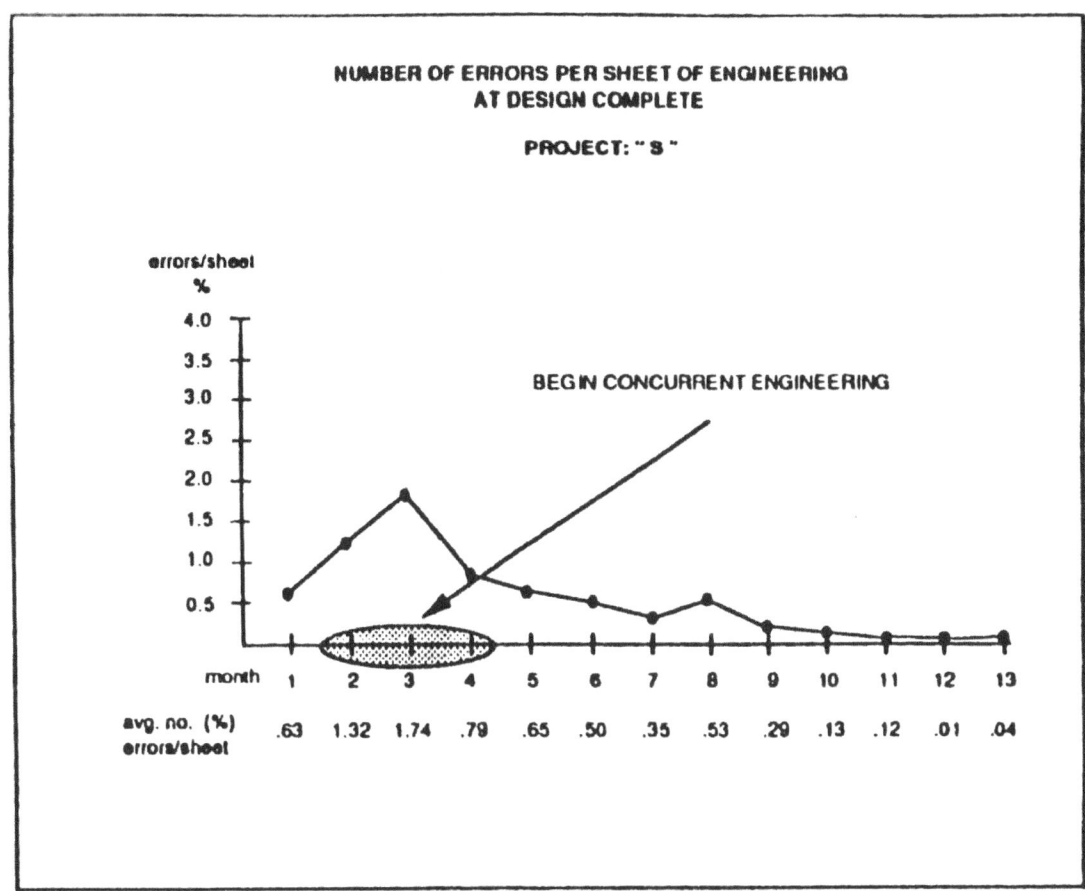

NUMBER OF ERRORS PER SHEET OF ENGINEERING
AT DESIGN COMPLETE

PROJECT: " S "

month	1	2	3	4	5	6	7	8	9	10	11	12	13
avg. no. (%) errors/sheet	.63	1.32	1.74	.79	.65	.50	.35	.53	.29	.13	.12	.01	.04

Figure 5

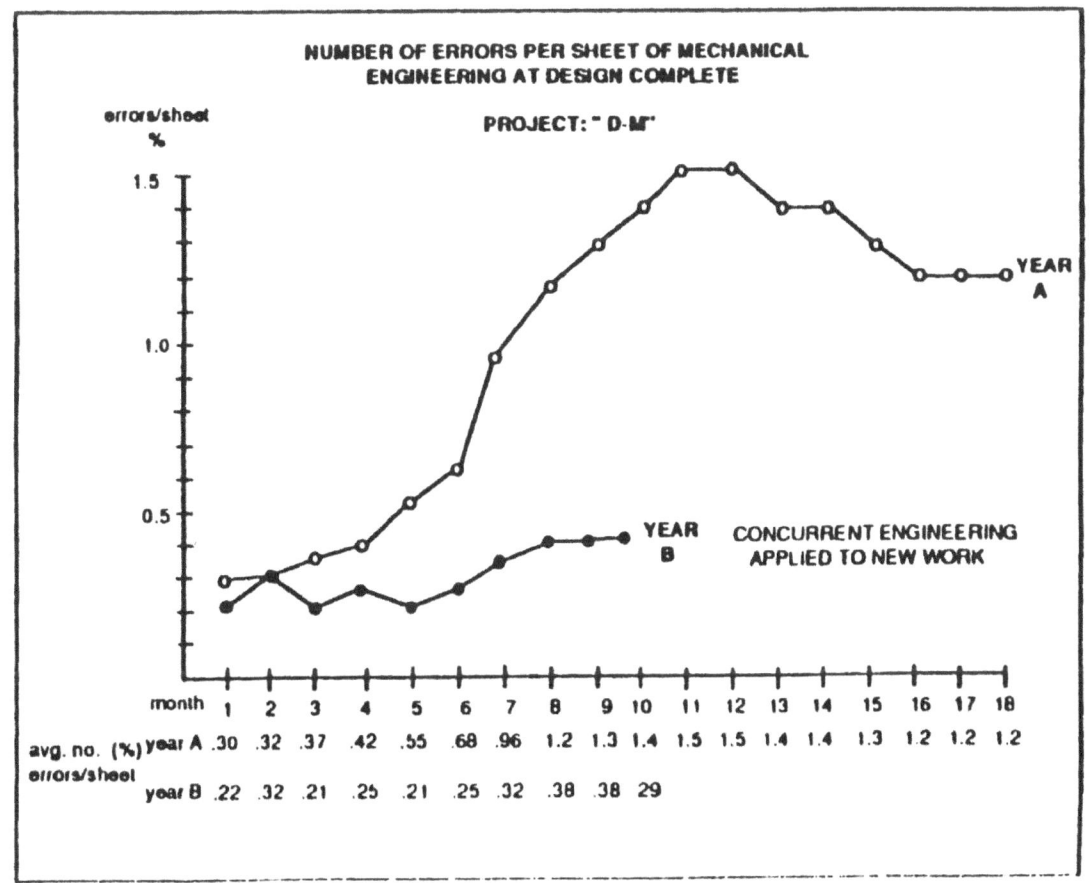

NUMBER OF ERRORS PER SHEET OF MECHANICAL
ENGINEERING AT DESIGN COMPLETE

PROJECT: " D-M"

month	1	2	3	4	5	6	7	8	9	10	11	12	13	14	15	16	17	18
avg. no. (%) errors/sheet year A	.30	.32	.37	.42	.55	.68	.96	1.2	1.3	1.4	1.5	1.5	1.4	1.4	1.3	1.2	1.2	1.2
year B	.22	.32	.21	.25	.21	.25	.32	.38	.38	29								

Figure 7

CONCLUSIONS

Why has management attempted so many changes? Why have some been successful while others have failed? Quite often, the answer lies in trying to implement a quick fix without giving proper consideration to all the factors which influence change.

The aerospace survey supported by various published documents showed that the difference between success and failure can be found in six Key Success Factors. These six factors aligned within three families of factors, and along with certain underlying conditions, serve as the basis for understanding the elements involved in successfully implementing a change within an aerospace company.

The Implementation Checklist questionnaire is an excellent tool for anyone charged with the responsibility of implementing a change. It can assist them in assuring that they have considered all the factors which may affect the change process.

The Concurrent Engineering example shows that a change stands a higher chance of being successfully implemented when proper consideration is given to the factors addressed in this paper. Failure to address these factors, however, can have a significantly negative impact on the process.

References

Bennis, W. (1989). <u>Why Leaders Can't Lead</u>. San Francisco: Jossey - Bass

Belgard, W. P., Fisher, K. K., & Rayner, S. R., (1988). Vision, Opportunity, Tenacity: Three Informal Processes That Influence Formal Transformation. In Kilmann, R. H., & Covin, T. J., (1988). <u>Corporate Transformation</u> (pp. 131-150). San Francisco: Jossey - Bass

Bolman, L.G., & Deal, T.E. (1984). <u>Modern Approaches to Understanding and Managing Organizations</u>. San Francisco: Jossey - Bass

Crosby, Philip b. (1979). <u>Quality is Free</u>. New York: New American Library.

Deming, W. Edwards. (1982). <u>Out of the Crisis</u>. Massachusetts: Massachusetts Institute of Technology.

Hambrick, L. G., & Joyce, W. F. <u>Organizational Adaption: Strategic Choice and Environmental Determinism</u>. In Administrative Science Quarterly, 1985, 30, (pp. 336-349)

Herzberg, F. , (1966). <u>Work of the Nature of Man</u>. Cleveland, Oh: World

Ishikawa, K. , (1987). <u>What is Total Quality Control? The Japanese Way</u>. Englewood Cliffs, NJ: Prentice-Hall

Juran, J, M. (1989). <u>Juran on Leadership for Quality; An Executive Handbook.</u> New York: The Free Press

Kiefer, C. F., & Stroh, P., (1984). A New Paradigm for Developing Organizations. In Adams, J. D. , (Ed.). (1984). <u>Transforming Work.</u> (pp. 171-181). Alexandria, Va : Miles River Press

McGill, Michael E., Ph.D. (1988). <u>American Management and the Quick Fix.</u> New York: Henry Holt and Co. Inc.

Mohrman, A. M. , Jr., Mohrman, S. A., Ledford, G. E., Jr., Cummings, T. G., Lawler, III E. E. & Associates. (1989). <u>Large-Scale Organizational Change</u>. San Francisco: Jossey - Bass

National Institute of Standards and Technology, The Malcolm Baldridge National Quality Award Consortium, Inc. Milwaukee, Wi.

Naisbitt, J., & Aburdene, P., (1990). <u>Megatrends 2000</u>. New York NY: William Morrow and Company, Inc.

Staff. (1990, October). Measuring the gap between the U.S. and Japanese auto makers. <u>Business Week,</u> p. 83

Szilagyi, A. D. , Jr., & Wallace, M. J., Jr., (1990). <u>Organizational Behavior and Performance (</u>5th ed.). Glenview. Il: Scott, Foresman and Company

Tichy, N.M., (1983).   Managing Strategic Change: Technical, Political &
   Cultural Dynamics. New York: John Wiley & Sons

Tichy, N.M. & Devanna, M. A., (1986).   The Transformational Leader.
   New York: John Wiley & Sons

White, O. W., (1981). Manufacturing Resource Planning: MRP II Unlocking
   America's Productivity Potential. Essex Junction, Vt: Oliver Wight
   Limited

Appendix A

Productivity Initiatives and Reasons Impacting Success

INITIATIVES

* MANAGERIAL GRID

* QUALITY CIRCLES

* T GROUPS

* MANAGEMENT BY OBJECTIVE

* ZERO DEFECTS

* PERT/CMP PLANNING

* THEORY Y / Z MANAGEMENT

* ZERO BASED BUDGETING

* MATRIX MANAGEMENT

* HIGH PERFORMANCE TEAMS

* PORTFOLIO MANAGEMENT

* REORGANIZATION

REASONS IMPACTING SUCCESS

* RESOURCE CONSTRAINTS (BUDGETS, PEOPLE, EQUIPMENT)

* POOR COMMUNICATIONS

* LACK OF MANAGEMENT ACCEPTANCE / COMMITMENT / RECOGNITION

* LITTLE OR NO TRAINING

* LACK OF MANAGEMENT PARTICIPATION / REINFORCEMENT

* ILL DEFINED PLANS / GOALS / OBJECTIVES

* ROLES AND RESPONSIBILITIES UNCLEAR / ACCOUNTABILITY

* NO WAY TO MEASURE PERFORMANCE / IMPROVEMENT

* NO ONE TO CHAMPION THE CAUSE - BE THE "TORCH BEARER"

* NO REWARD OR RECOGNITION OF PERFORMANCE

* CORPORATE CULTURE NOT WILLING TO ACCEPT CHANGE

* NO WORK FORCE BUY IN

* WRONG MANAGEMENT STYLE / APPROACH

* NO RISK ASSESSMENT / ANALYSIS

* ORGANIZATION NOT STRUCTURED FOR CHANGE

* PRACTICES AND PROCEDURES NOT GENERATED OR REVISED TO SUPPORT THE CHANGE

Appendix B

Aerospace survey Questionnaire

PLEASE READ THIS ENTIRE PAGE BEFORE ANSWERING!!

DOES YOUR COMPANY EMPLOY A MATRIX ORGANIZATION
STRUCTURE?
YES___ NO___

PLEASE IDENTIFY THE NUMBER OF MAJOR INITIATIVES (OR CHANGES)
YOUR COMPANY HAS INTRODUCED IN THE LAST 3 YEARS BY CATEGORY.

EXAMPLES OF MAJOR INITIATIVES ARE:

QUALITY CIRCLES,   MRP II,   JUST-IN-TIME,   MATRIX MGMT.,   HIGH PERFORMANCE
WORK TEAMS, PROCESS SIMPLIFICATIONS,   SIGNIFICANT REORGANIZATIONS,
PERFORMANCE IMPROVEMENTS

CATEGORY	NUMBER OF INITIATIVES
A. HIGHLY SUCCESSFUL	_____
B. SOMEWHAT SUCCESSFUL	_____
C. UNSUCCESSFUL	_____
D. TOTAL INITIATIVES	_____

(**D.** SHOULD EQUAL THE SUM OF **A. B. & C.** ABOVE)

CATEGORY	SAMPLE CRITERIA
HIGHLY SUCCESSFUL	SIGNIFICANT PRODUCTIVITY GAINS USED FOR A SIGNIFICANT TIME ACCEPTED BY THE WORK FORCE
SOMEWHAT SUCCESSFUL	EXPECTED GAINS REALIZED MODERATE USAGE OVER TIME WORK FORCE NEUTRAL
UNSUCCESSFUL	LITTLE OR NO GAIN REALIZED MINIMAL OR NO UTILIZATION WORK FORCE WAS NEGATIVE

NOW THINK ABOUT AN INITIATIVE IN EACH CATEGORY THAT STANDS OUT THE MOST TO YOU.

PLEASE COMPLETE <u>ONE</u> QUESTIONNAIRE FOR <u>EACH OF THESE INITIATIVES</u>.

USE THE __**GREEN**__ COLOR PAGES FOR THE **HIGHLY SUCCESSFUL**

USE THE _ **YELLOW**_ COLOR PAGES FOR THE **MODERATELY SUCCESSFUL**

USE THE __**ROSE**___ COLOR PAGES FOR THE **UNSUCCESSFUL**

NOTE: IF YOU FEEL A QUESTION DOES NOT APPLY IN THE QUESTIONNAIRE PLEASE INDICATE WITH A "N/A" IN THE MARGIN TO THE LEFT OF THE QUESTION!

HIGHLY SUCCESSFUL

TITLE OF THE INITIATIVE: _____

BRIEF DESCRIPTION:

A1. WHO INTRODUCED THIS INITIATIVE?
COMPANY PRES. __   COMPANY V.P. __   DIRECTOR __   MANAGER __
CUSTOMER ___   EMPLOYEES ___   OTHER _____

A2. WAS THIS PERSON FROM:
A CENTRAL SUPPORT ORGANIZATION   ____
A PROGRAM OR PRODUCT AREA   ____

A3. DID THIS PERSON HAVE LEAD RESPONSIBILITY FOR THE
IMPLEMENTATION?
YES___ NO___

A4. IF NO, WHAT ORGANIZATION DID? _____

A5. DID SENIOR MANAGEMENT PLAY AN ACTIVE ROLL IN
IMPLEMENTATION?
(i.e.. ATTEND MEETINGS, ALLOCATE RESOURCES, ETC.)
YES___ NO___

A6. WAS A FUNDAMENTAL CHANGE IN MANAGEMENT STYLE REQUIRED?
YES___ NO___

A7. WAS THE PURPOSE / OBJECTIVE OF THE INITIATIVE CLEARLY
IDENTIFIED TO:
SR. MGMT.   YES___ NO___
MIDDLE MGMT.   YES___ NO___
GENERAL POPULATION YES___ NO___

B1. APPROXIMATELY HOW MANY PEOPLE WORKED ON THIS INITIATIVE?

_____

B2. OF THIS NUMBER WHAT % :
WERE ASSIGNED FULL TIME _____
SUPPORTED PART TIME _____

B3. HOW MUCH LATITUDE WAS ALLOWED THE IMPLEMENTATION TEAM?
_____ AUTONOMOUS OPERATION
_____ GIVEN GENERAL BOUNDARY CONDITIONS AND CONSTRAINTS
_____ GIVEN SPECIFIC DIRECTION WITHIN A STRUCTURED PLAN

B4. HOW DID YOU COMMUNICATE THIS INITIATIVE?
___ SR. MGMT. ANNOUNCEMENT   ___ COMPANY NEWSLETTER
___ LARGE ORG. STAFF MTG.   ___ SMALL STAFF MEETINGS
___ VIDEO TAPE PRESENTATIONS OTHER:_____

C1. WAS FUNDING ($) INITIALLY ALLOCATED TO THIS INITIATIVE?
YES___ NO___

C2. DID YOU RECEIVE THE FUNDING YOU ORIGINALLY REQUESTED?
YES___ NO___

C3. WAS THE FUNDING INCREASED PRIOR TO FULL IMPLEMENTATION?
YES___ NO___

C4. WAS THE FUNDING DECREASED PRIOR TO FULL IMPLEMENTATION?
YES___ NO___

D1. WERE NEW OR ADDITIONAL FACILITIES REQUIRED FOR THIS
INITIATIVE?
YES___ NO___

D2. WERE ANY FACILITY MODIFICATIONS REQUIRED?
YES___ NO___

D3. WERE THE FACILITY MODIFICATIONS MADE?
YES___ NO___

E1. WAS ADDITIONAL COMPUTER HARDWARE REQUIRED FOR THIS
INITIATIVE?
YES___ NO___

E2. WAS THE ADDITIONAL COMPUTER HARDWARE OBTAINED?
YES___ NO___

E3. WAS ADDITIONAL COMPUTER SOFTWARE REQUIRED FOR THIS
INITIATIVE?
YES___ NO___

E4. WAS THE ADDITIONAL COMPUTER SOFTWARE OBTAINED?
YES___ NO___

F1. WHY WAS THIS INITIATIVE UNDERTAKEN?
(WRITE IN (P) FOR THE PRIMARY REASON AND (S) FOR THE SECONDARY REASON)

___ RESPONSE TO CHANGES IN INDUSTRY
___ COMPLY WITH GOVERNMENT DIRECTION
___ INCORPORATE STATE OF THE ART TECHNOLOGY
___ ENHANCE COMPETITIVE POSITION
___ IMPROVE SAFETY
___ RESPONSE TO A CRISIS
___ RESPOND TO EMPLOYEES NEEDS OR REQUEST
___ REDUCE OPERATING COSTS
___ EXPAND INTO NEW PRODUCT LINE
___ OTHER _____

F2. DID THE INITIATIVE HAVE MGMT. APPROVAL PRIOR TO
IMPLEMENTATION?
YES___ NO___

F3. DID ANYONE CONSIDER IMPACTS TO CURRENT OPERATIONS?
YES___ NO___

F4. WAS A DETAIL IMPLEMENTATION PLAN DEVELOPED?
YES___ NO___

G1. WAS A COMPLETION DATE ESTABLISHED FOR IMPLEMENTATION?
YES___ NO___

G2. AGAINST THE ORIGINAL IMPLEMENTATION DATE, WAS THE
INITIATIVE:
COMPLETED AHEAD OF SCHEDULE ____
COMPLETED CLOSE TO SCHEDULE ____
SIGNIFICANTLY BEHIND SCHEDULE ____

H1. DID YOU PROVIDE TRAINING TO SUPPORT THIS INITIATIVE?
YES___ NO___

H2. IF YES, FOR WHAT PURPOSE WAS THE TRAINING INTENDED?
___ INFORM / INSTRUCT EMPLOYEES HOW TO USE THE NEW
METHOD
___ MODIFY BEHAVIOR / CULTURAL CHANGE
___ GOVERNMENT REQUIREMENT

I1. WERE PROCEDURES AFFECTED BY THIS CHANGE?
   YES___ NO___

I2. WERE PROCEDURES WRITTEN SPECIFICALLY TO IMPLEMENT THIS
    INITIATIVE?
   YES___ NO___

I3. WERE PROCEDURES MODIFIED TO SUPPORT IMPLEMENTATION?
   YES___ NO___

J1. WAS A REWARD / RECOGNITION PROGRAM ESTABLISHED
    SPECIFICALLY FOR
    THIS INITIATIVE?
   YES___ NO___

J2. IF YES, WHOM DID IT REWARD?
   ____ INDIVIDUALS ____ GROUPS ____ BOTH ____

J3. IF NO, DID YOU REWARD PERFORMANCE UNDER EXISTING
    METHODS?
   YES___ NO___

J4. WAS PARTICIPATION IN THIS INITIATIVE DOCUMENTED IN THE
    EMPLOYEES
    PERFORMANCE APPRAISAL REVIEW?
   YES___ NO___

K1. WAS A CONSULTANT INVOLVED IN THIS INITIATIVE?
   YES___ NO___

K2. IF YES, IDENTIFY THE FUNCTION PERFORMED.
    (CHECK AS MANY AS APPLY)
    ____ TRAINING   ____ EVALUATION
    ____ IMPLEMENTATION   ____ CERTIFICATION
    ____ OPERATIONS   OTHER _____

L1. WAS AN ORGANIZATIONAL RESTRUCTURING REQUIRED TO SUPPORT
    THIS
    INITIATIVE?
   YES___ NO___

L2. DID AN ORGANIZATIONAL RESTRUCTURE OCCUR BECAUSE OF THIS
    INITIATIVE?
   YES___ NO___

L3. IN YOUR VIEW, HAS THERE BEEN A PERMANENT CHANGE TO HOW
    YOUR COMPANY DOES BUSINESS BECAUSE OF THIS INITIATIVE?
   YES___ NO___

IF YOU HAD IT TO DO OVER AGAIN, WHAT WOULD YOU DO DIFFERENTLY?

_____

_____

_____

_____

_____

_____

_____

_____

_____

_____

_____

_____

_____

_____

_____

_____

THANKS FOR TAKING THE TIME TO COMPLETE THIS QUESTIONNAIRE!!

Appendix C

Aerospace survey Summary

		SUCCESSFUL INITIATIVE	UNSUCCESSFUL IMPLEMENTATION
INITIATIVE INTRODUCTION	MATRIX	* PRES. OR VP INTRODUCED THE INITIATIVE MOST OFTEN -FOLLOWED BY MANAGERS AND THAN DIRECTORS * ONE THIRD WERE INTRODUCED IN PRODUCT AREAS * LEAD RESPONSIBILITY FREQUENTLY FELL TO THE INITIATOR	* PRES. OR VP INTRODUCED HALF OF THE INITIATIVES * NONE WERE INTRODUCED IN PRODUCT AREAS * LEAD RESPONSIBILITY FELL TO THE INITIATOR -MORE OFTEN THAN IN THE SUCCESSFUL CASES
	NON-MATRIX	* ONLY THE PRES. OR VP INTRODUCED THE INITIATIVE * NONE WERE INTRODUCED BY PRODUCT AREAS * LEAD RESPONSIBILITY FREQUENTLY FELL TO THE INITIATOR	* ONLY THE PRES. OR VP INTRODUCED THE INITIATIVE * NONE WERE INTRODUCED BY PRODUCT AREAS * LEAD RESP. ALWAYS FELL TO THE INITIATOR
SENIOR MANAGEMENT	MATRIX	* SR. MGMT. PLAYED AN ACTIVE ROLE IN VIRTUALLY ALL OF THE IMPLEMENTATIONS * TWO-THIRDS REQUIRED A FUNDAMENTAL CHANGE TO THEIR MGMT. STYLE	* SR. MGMT. PLAYED AN ACTIVE ROLE IN ONLY HALF OF THE IMPLEMENTATIONS * TWO-THIRDS REQUIRED A FUNDAMENTAL CHANGE TO THEIR MGMT. STYLE
	NON-MATRIX	* SR. MGMT. PLAYED AN ACTIVE ROLE IN ALL OF THE IMPLEMENTATIONS * EVERY CASE REQUIRED A FUNDAMENTAL CHANGE TO THEIR MGMT. STYLE	* SR. MGMT. PLAYED AN ACTIVE ROLE IN ONLY HALF OF THE IMPLEMENTATIONS * ONLY ONE-FOURTH OF THE CASES INDICATED A REQUIREMENT FOR A FUNDAMENTAL STYLE CHANGE

WORK FORCE PARTICIPATION

	SUCCESSFUL INITIATIVE	UNSUCCESSFUL IMPLEMENTATION
MATRIX	* THE NUMBER OF PEOPLE PARTICIPATING WAS EVENLY DISTRIBUTED (AS A %) IN FOUR POPULATION GROUPS: 1-20, 21-49, 50-100, 101-500 * GREATER THAN 55% WERE ASSIGNED PART TIME	* THE NO. OF PEOPLE PARTICIPATING WAS EVENLY DISTRIBUTED (AS A %) IN THREE GROUPS: 1-20, 21-49, 50-100, * 50% WERE ASSIGNED PART TIME
NON-MATRIX	* THOSE RESPONDING TO THIS SECTION DID NOT HAVE DATA AS TO HOW MANY PEOPLE WERE INVOLVED AND IF THEY WERE ASSIGNED FULL OR PART TIME.	* THE NO. OF PEOPLE PARTICIPATING WAS CONCENTRATED IN THE 1-20 GROUP. * 66% WERE ASSIGNED PART TIME

BOUNDARY CONDITIONS

	SUCCESSFUL INITIATIVE	UNSUCCESSFUL IMPLEMENTATION

MATRIX	* 38% AUTONOMOUS OPERATIONS
	  38% GENERAL BOUNDARY CONDITIONS
	  24% SPECIFIC DIRECTIONS
		* 33% AUTONOMOUS OPERATIONS
		  34% GENERAL BOUNDARY CONDITIONS
		  33% SPECIFIC DIRECTIONS

NON-MATRIX	* 0% AUTONOMOUS OPERATIONS
	  25% GENERAL BOUNDARY CONDITIONS
	  75% SPECIFIC DIRECTIONS
		* 25% AUTONOMOUS OPERATIONS
		  25% GENERAL BOUNDARY CONDITIONS
		  50% SPECIFIC DIRECTIONS

	SUCCESSFUL INITIATIVE	UNSUCCESSFUL IMPLEMENTATION
COMMUNICATIONS		
MATRIX	* THE INITIATIVE WAS CLEARLY IDENTIFIED TO: SR. MGMT. 93% OF THE TIME MID. MGMT. 86% OF THE TIME WORK FORCE 53% OF THE TIME * COMMUNICATIONS TOOLS WERE (IN ORDER OF FREQUENCY): SR. MGMT. ANNOUNCEMENT, LG. STAFF, CO. NEWS, SMALL STAFF, VIDEO PRESENTATIONS	* THE INITIATIVE WAS CLEARLY IDENTIFIED TO: SR. MGMT. 78% OF THE TIME MID. MGMT. 56% OF THE TIME WORK FORCE 33% OF THE TIME * COMMUNICATIONS TOOLS WERE (IN ORDER OF FREQUENCY): SR. MGMT. ANNOUNCEMENT, LG. STAFF, SMALL STAFF, CO. NEWS, NO VIDEO PRESENTATIONS
NON-MATRIX	* THE INITIATIVE WAS CLEARLY IDENTIFIED TO ALL LEVEL IN VIRTUALLY EVERY CASE. * INFORMATION WAS EVENLY DISTRIBUTED VIA: SR. MGMT. ANNOUNCEMENT, LG. STAFF, CO. NEWS, SMALL STAFF, VIDEO PRESENTATIONS	* THE INITIATIVE WAS CLEARLY IDENTIFIED TO: SR. MGMT. 50% OF THE TIME MID. MGMT. 75% OF THE TIME WORK FORCE 75% OF THE TIME * COMMUNICATIONS TOOLS WERE (IN ORDER OF FREQUENCY): CO. NEWS, SR. MGMT. ANNOUNCEMENT, SMALL STAFF, LG. STAFF, VIDEO PRESENTATION (ONE CASE)
TRAINING		
MATRIX	* THREE-FOURTHS OF THE RESPONDERS PROVIDED TRAINING. * THE PURPOSE OF THE TRAINING WAS TO: 1). MODIFY BEHAVIOR OR CHANGE CULTURE 2). INFORMATION AND OR INSTRUCTIONAL	* ONE HALF OF THE RESPONDERS PROVIDED TRAINING. * THE PURPOSE OF THE TRNG. WAS EVENLY SPLIT: 1). MODIFY BEHAVIOR OR CHANGE CULTURE 2). INFORMATION AND OR INSTRUCTIONAL
NON-MATRIX	* DATA FOR THIS GROUP WAS THE SAME AS THE MATRIX RESPONSES.	* TRAINING WAS PROVIDED IN ONE HALF ON THE CASES TO INFORM AND INSTRUCT ONLY.

FUNDING

	SUCCESSFUL INITIATIVE	UNSUCCESSFUL IMPLEMENTATION

MATRIX	* FUNDING WAS REQUESTED IN HALF OF THE CASES.
	  - ONE HALF OF THOSE REQUESTS WERE GRANTED.
	  - A THIRD RECEIVED ADDITIONAL FUNDS.
	  - NO DECREASES IN FUNDING WERE REPORTED.
		* FUNDING WAS REQUESTED IN 44% OF THE CASES.
		  - THREE FOURTHS OF THE REQ'S WERE GRANTED.
		  - A CASE RECEIVED ADDITIONAL FUNDS.
		  - NO DECREASES IN FUNDING WERE REPORTED.

NON-MATRIX	* FUNDING WAS REQUESTED IN ONLY ONE CASE
	  - THE REQUEST WAS GRANTED.
	  - NO ADDITIONAL FUNDING WAS ALLOCATED.
	  - A FUNDING DECREASE WAS REPORTED.
		* FUNDING WAS REQUESTED IN 75% OF THE CASES.
		  - ONE HALF OF THOSE REQUESTS WERE GRANTED.
		  - NO ADDITIONAL FUNDING WAS ALLOCATED.
		  - A FUNDING DECREASE WAS REPORTED IN ONE CASE.

FACILITIES

	SUCCESSFUL INITIATIVE	UNSUCCESSFUL IMPLEMENTATION

MATRIX	* ONE FIFTH OF THE CASES REQUIRED ADD'L. SPACE.
	* ONE FIFTH REQUIRED MODIFICATIONS.
	  ALL MODIFICATION REQUESTS WERE GRANTED.
		* ONE THIRD OF THE CASES REQUIRED ADD'L. SPACE
		* ONE THIRD REQUIRED MODIFICATIONS.
		  ALL MODIFICATION REQUESTS WERE GRANTED.

NON-MATRIX	* NO ADDITIONAL SPACE REQUIREMENTS WERE REPORTED FOR THIS GROUP.
	* ONE THIRD REQUIRED MODIFICATIONS.
	  ALL MODIFICATION REQUESTS WERE GRANTED.
		* NO ADDITIONAL SPACE REQUIREMENTS WERE REPORTED FOR THIS GROUP.
		* ONE FOURTH REQUIRED MODIFICATIONS.
		  ALL MODIFICATION REQUESTS WERE GRANTED.

Appendix C

TOOLS

SUCCESSFUL INITIATIVE

MATRIX
* 27% RESPONDED ADDITIONAL H/W WAS REQUIRED.
* 75% OF THE REQUESTS WERE GRANTED.
* 47% RESPONDED NEEDING ADDITIONAL S/W. ALL REQUESTS WERE GRANTED.

NON-MATRIX
* NO REQUESTS FOR ADDITIONAL H/W WERE RECEIVED.
* NO ADDITIONAL EQUIPMENT WAS PROCURED.
* 33% RESPONDED NEEDING ADDITIONAL S/W. ALL REQUESTS WERE GRANTED.

UNSUCCESSFUL IMPLEMENTATION

MATRIX
* 45% RESPONDED ADD'L H/W WAS REQUIRED.
* 75% OF THE REQUESTS WERE GRANTED.
* 33% RESPONDED NEEDING ADDITIONAL S/W. 75% OF THE REQUESTS WERE GRANTED.

NON-MATRIX
* NO REQUESTS FOR ADD'L H/W WERE RECEIVED.
* NO ADDITIONAL EQUIPMENT WAS PROCURED.
* 50% RESPONDED NEEDING ADDITIONAL S/W. ALL REQUESTS WERE GRANTED.

REASON FOR CHANGE

SUCCESSFUL INITIATIVE

MATRIX
* PRIMARY OBJECTIVES WERE TO:
1) IMPROVE COMPETITIVE POSITION
2) REDUCE OPERATING COSTS
3) ALIGN WITH CHANGES IN INDUSTRY
4) RESPOND TO REQUEST FROM EMPLOYEES

NON-MATRIX
* PRIMARY OBJECTIVES WERE TO:
1) RESPOND TO REQUEST FROM EMPLOYEES
2) IMPROVE COMPETITIVE POSITION
3) REDUCE OPERATING COSTS
4) IMPROVE STATE-OF-THE-ART TECHNOLOGY

UNSUCCESSFUL IMPLEMENTATION

MATRIX
* PRIMARY OBJECTIVES WERE TO:
1) IMPROVE COMPETITIVE POSITION
2) REDUCE OPERATING COSTS
3) RESPOND TO GOVERNMENT DIRECTION
4) RESPOND TO CRISIS

NON-MATRIX
* PRIMARY OBJECTIVES WERE TO:
1) IMPROVE COMPETITIVE POSITION
2) REDUCE OPERATING COSTS
3) RESPOND TO CRISIS
4) RESPOND TO REQUEST FROM EMPLOYEES

PLANNING

	SUCCESSFUL INITIATIVE	UNSUCCESSFUL IMPLEMENTATION
MATRIX	* IMPACTS TO CURRENT OPERATIONS (RISK) WAS CONSIDERED IN ALL CASES. * 87% OF THE CASES DEVELOPED DETAIL IMPL. PLANS * 64% ESTABLISHED COMPLETION DATES. * 74% REPORTED COMPLETION CLOSE TO PLANNED DATE	* 70% CONSIDERED IMPACTS (RISK) TO CURRENT OPERATIONS. * 50% OF THE CASES DEVELOPED DETAIL IMPL. PLANS * 33% ESTABLISHED COMPLETION DATES. * 50% WERE COMPLETED CLOSE TO PLANNED DATE
NON-MATRIX	* IMPACTS TO CURRENT OPERATIONS (RISK) WAS CONSIDERED IN ALL CASES. * 100% OF THE CASES DEVELOPED DETAIL IMPL. PLANS * 100% ESTABLISHED COMPLETION DATES. * 100% WERE COMPLETED CLOSE TO PLANNED DATE	* 75% CONSIDERED IMPACTS (RISK) TO CURRENT OPERATIONS. * 25% OF THE CASES DEVELOPED DETAIL IMPL. PLANS * 33% ESTABLISHED COMPLETION DATES. * 50% COMPLETED CLOSE TO PLANNED DATE

POLICIES & PROCEDURES

	SUCCESSFUL INITIATIVE	UNSUCCESSFUL IMPLEMENTATION
MATRIX	* 73% INDICATED PROCEDURES WERE AFFECTED * 36% WROTE NEW PROCEDURES * 79% MODIFIED PROCEDURES	* 56% INDICATED PROCEDURES WERE AFFECTED * 33% WROTE NEW PROCEDURES * 44% MODIFIED PROCEDURES
NON-MATRIX	* 73% INDICATED PROCEDURES WERE AFFECTED * 36% WROTE NEW PROCEDURES * 79% MODIFIED PROCEDURES	* 75% INDICATED PROCEDURES WERE AFFECTED * 50% WROTE NEW PROCEDURES * 67% MODIFIED PROCEDURES

REWARD & RECOGNITION

	SUCCESSFUL INITIATIVE	UNSUCCESSFUL IMPLEMENTATION
MATRIX	* 57% ESTABLISHED A SPECIFIC REWARD PROGRAM * 87% RECOGNIZED BOTH INDIVIDUALS & GROUPS * ONE HALF OF THOSE WHO DID NOT SET UP A NEW PROG GAVE RECOGNITION UNDER THEIR CURRENT SYSTEM. * 80% DOCUMENTED PARTICIPATION IN THE EMPLOYEE APPRAISAL REVIEWS	* 11% ESTABLISIIED A SPECIFIC REWARD PROGRAM * ONLY INDIVIDUALS RECEIVED RECOGNITION * HALF OF THOSE WHO DID NOT SET UP A NEW PROG. GAVE RECOGNITION UNDER THEIR CURRENT SYSTEM. * 22% DOCUMENTED PARTICIPATION IN THE EMPLOYEE APPRAISAL REVIEWS
NON-MATRIX	* 25% ESTABLISIIED A SPECIFIC REWARD PROGRAM * INDIVIDUALS WERE RECOGNIZED UNDER EXISTING SYS.'s * 75% DOCUMENTED PARTICIPATION IN THE EMPLOYEE APPRAISAL REVIEWS	* NONE ESTABLISHED A SPECIFIC REWARD PROGRAM * RECOGNITION OF ANY TYPE WAS NOT KNOWN * NOT DOCUMENTED ON EMPLOYEE EVALUATION FORM

CONSULTANTS

	SUCCESSFUL INITIATIVE	UNSUCCESSFUL IMPLEMENTATION
MATRIX	* 21% UTILIZED CONSULTANTS * PRIMARY PURPOSES WERE TO EVALUATE AND TRAIN	* 56% UTILIZED CONSULTANTS * PRIMARY PURPOSES WERE TO IMPLEMENT, TRAIN, AND EVALUATE
NON-MATRIX	* 50% UTILIZED CONSULTANTS * PRIMARY PURPOSES WERE TO TRAIN, EVALUATE AND IMPLEMENT	* 75% UTILIZED CONSULTANTS * PRIMARY PURPOSES WERE TO TRAIN, IMPLEMENT, AND EVALUATE

ORGANIZATIONAL RESTRUCTURING

	SUCCESSFUL INITIATIVE	UNSUCCESSFUL IMPLEMENTATION
MATRIX	* ONE THIRD REPORTED A RESTRUCTURING WAS NECESSARY FOR IMPLEMENTATION * 75% REPORTED A RESTRUCTURING CAME ABOUT BECAUSE OF THIS CHANGE	* ONE THIRD REPORTED A RESTRUCTURING WAS NECESSARY FOR IMPLEMENTATION * 38% REPORTED A RESTRUCTURING CAME ABOUT BECAUSE OF THIS CHANGE
NON-MATRIX	* ONE THIRD REPORTED A RESTRUCTURING WAS NECESSARY FOR IMPLEMENTATION * 33% REPORTED A RESTRUCTURING CAME ABOUT BECAUSE OF THIS CHANGE	* ONE HALF REPORTED A RESTRUCTURING WAS NECESSARY FOR IMPLEMENTATION * 50% REPORTED A RESTRUCTURING CAME ABOUT BECAUSE OF THIS CHANGE

APPENDIX D PRESENTATION

IMPLEMENTING CHANGE:

THE DYNAMICS OF THE CHANGE PROCESS IN THE

AEROSPACE INDUSTRY

IMPLEMENTING CHANGE

"There is nothing more difficult to take in hand,

more perilous to conduct, or more uncertain in its

success than to take the lead in the introduction of

a new order of things."

W. EDWARDS DEMING, Ph.D

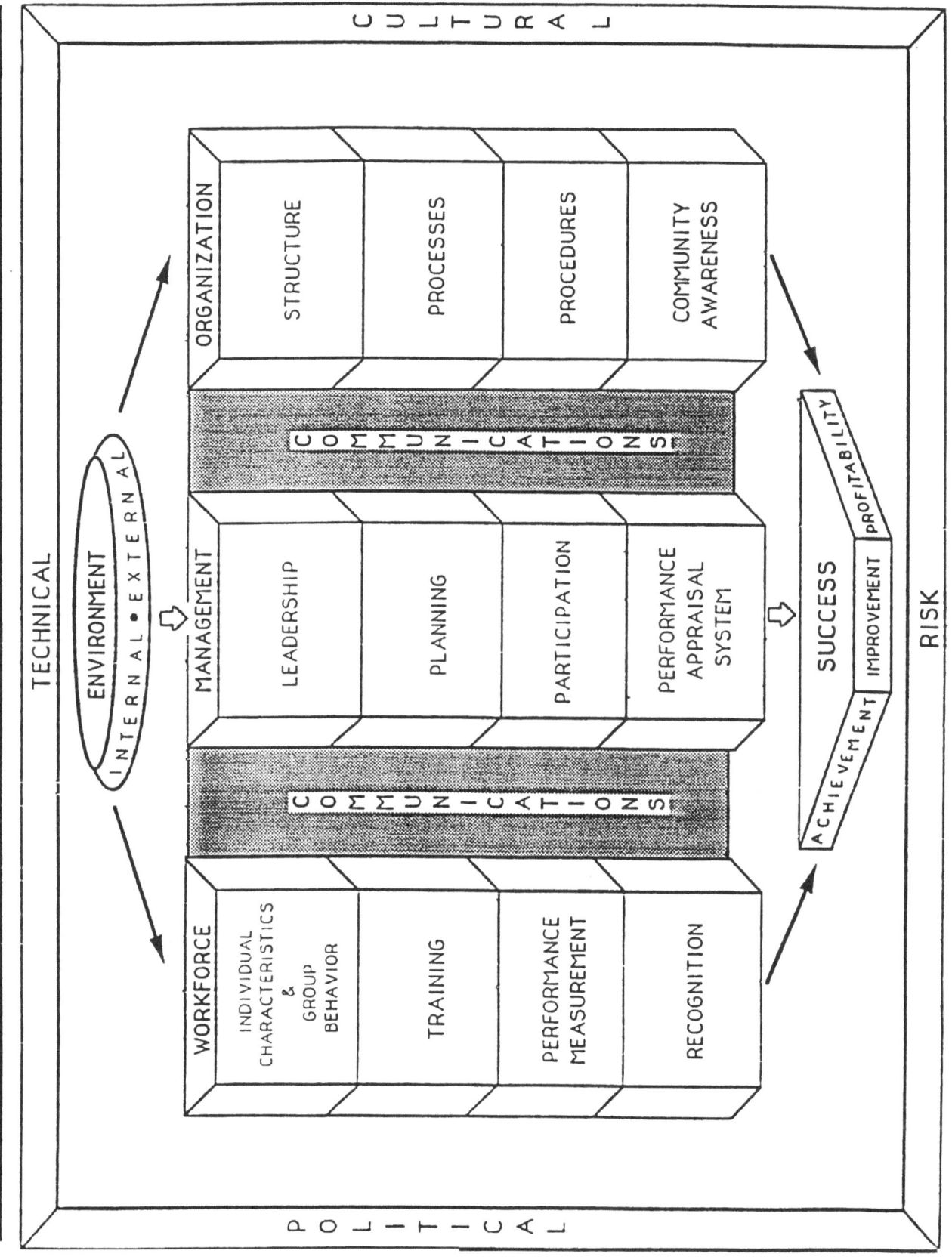

FACTORS INFLUENCING CHANGE MODEL

IMPLEMENTING CHANGE

KEY SUCCESS FACTORS

ACTION SEQUENCE

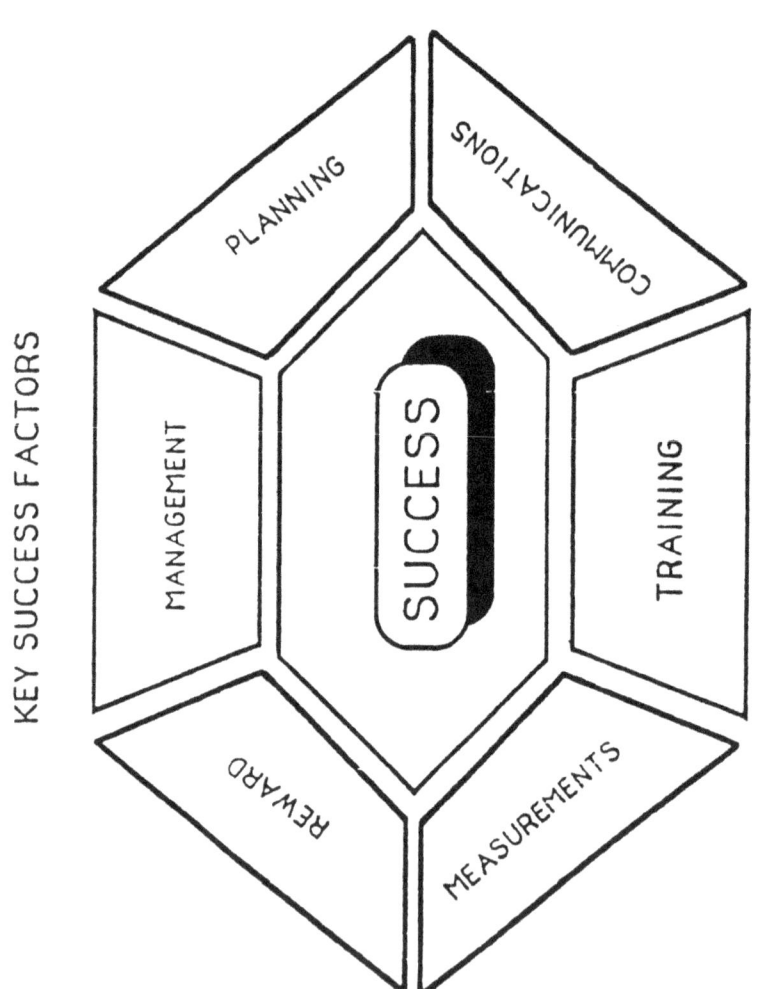

PLANNING

COMMUNICATIONS

MANAGEMENT

SUCCESS

TRAINING

REWARD

MEASUREMENTS

MANAGEMENT

IMPLEMENTING CHANGE

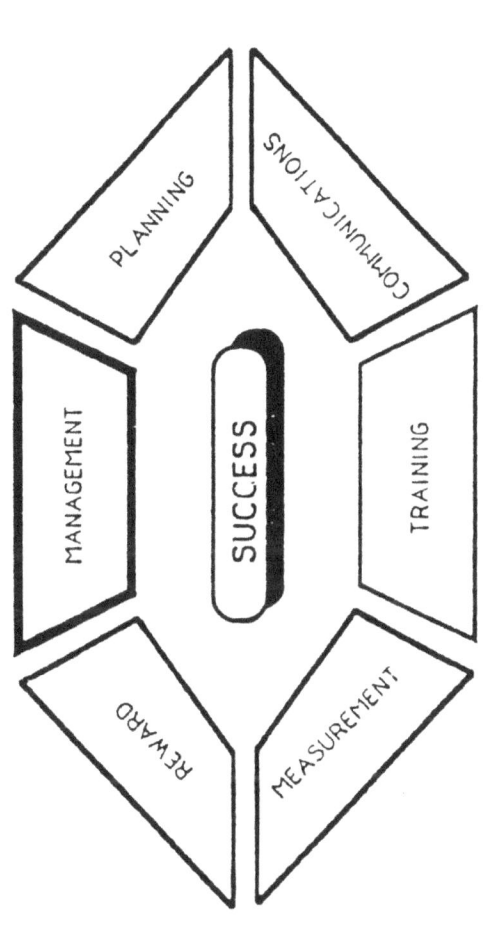

KEY SUCCESS FACTORS

O   SENIOR MANAGEMENT SHOULD INITIATE THE CHANGE

O   ACTIVELY PARTICIPATE IN THE ACTIVITY

O   BE ABLE TO EXCITE THE WORK FORCE

O   BE AWARE OF ALL FACTORS WHICH INFLUENCE CHANGE

O   DEVELOP THE REWARD AND RECOGNITION PROGRAM

IMPLEMENTING CHANGE

PLANNING

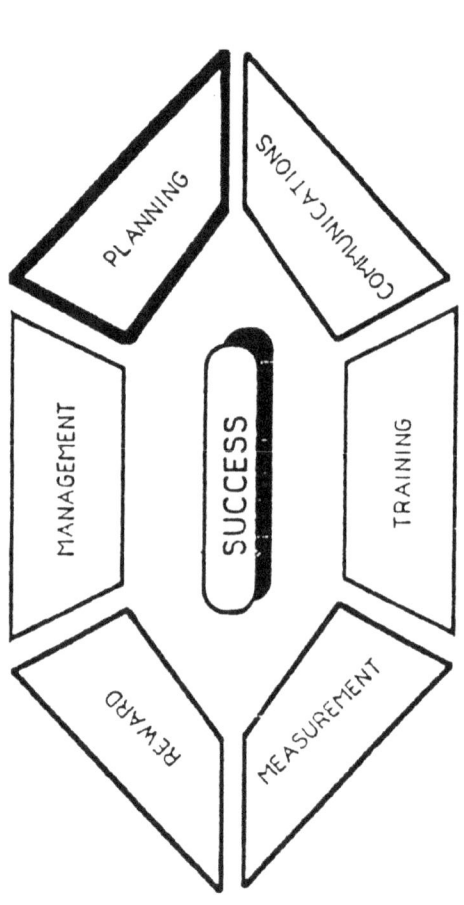

KEY SUCCESS FACTORS

o   SUCCESS IS CONTINGENT UPON A STRUCTURED PLAN

o   UNDERSTAND AND MITIGATE RISK

o   UNDERSTAND THE CORPORATE CULTURE

o   UTILIZE AN IMPLEMENTATION CHECKLIST

o   DEVELOP AND IMPLEMENT ON A "PILOT" PROGRAM

o   RECOGNIZE "TERTIARY" RELATIONSHIPS

COMMUNICATIONS

IMPLEMENTING CHANGE

KEY SUCCESS FACTORS

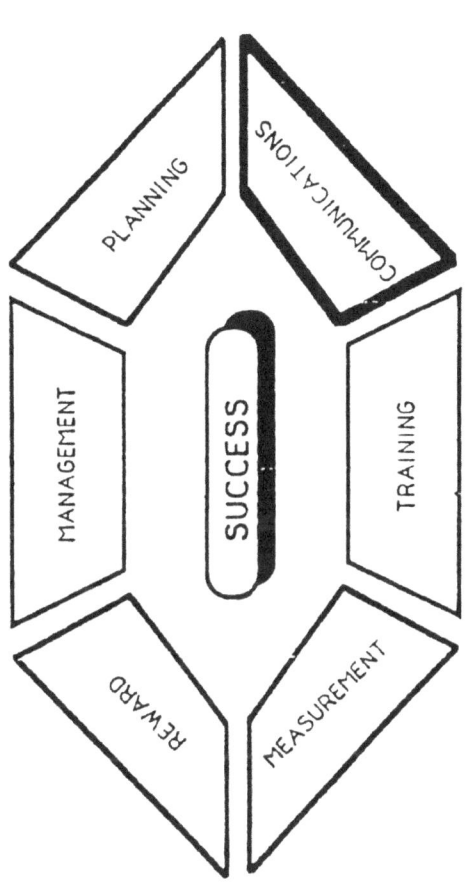

o   LINKS ALL FACTORS TOGETHER

o   UTILIZE ALL FORMS OF MEDIA AVAILABLE

o   CLEARLY STATE GOALS AND OBJECTIVES

o   COMPLEX ISSUE IN MAJOR ORGANIZATIONS

o   CRITICAL TO WORK FORCE BUY-IN

TRAINING

KEY SUCCESS FACTORS

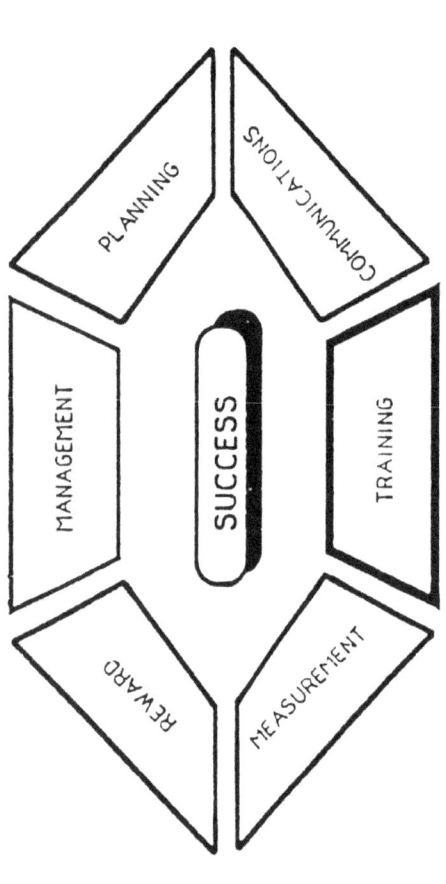

PLANNING
COMMUNICATIONS
MANAGEMENT
SUCCESS
TRAINING
REWARD
MEASUREMENT

IMPLEMENTING CHANGE

o MOST UNDER ESTIMATED, UNDER BUDGETED, & LEAST UNDERSTOOD FACTOR

o EXCUSES FOR NOT TRAINING ARE NUMEROUS

o "QUALITY OF THE PRODUCT IS A DIRECT REFLECTION OF THE AMOUNT OF TRAINING GIVEN TO THE PARTICIPATING WORK FORCE"

o IMPLEMENTATION OF NEW PROCESSES REQUIRES TRAINING

o CONSISTENCY OF APPLICATION IS ACHIEVED IN DOCUMENTING AND EDUCATING THE WORK FORCE TO COMPANY PROCEDURES

MEASUREMENTS

KEY SUCCESS FACTORS

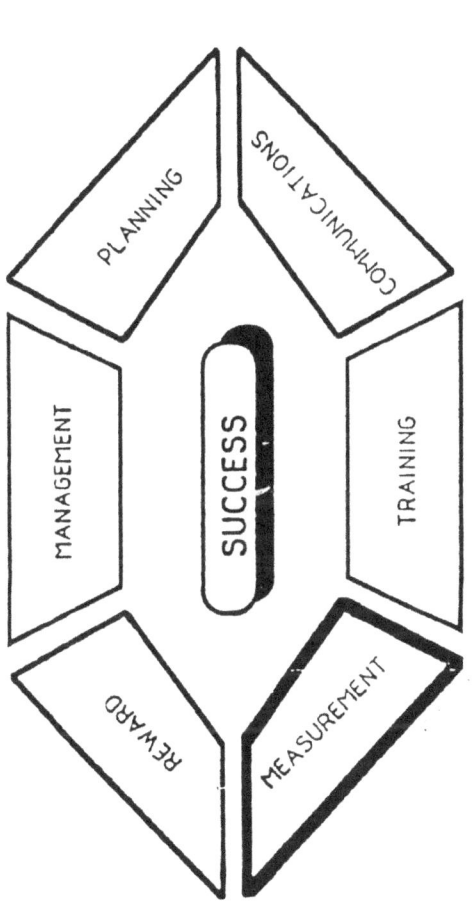

o MEASUREMENTS LEAD TO IMPROVEMENT

o USE APPROPRIATE & MEANINGFUL MEASUREMENTS

o WORK FORCE PARTICIPATION & BUY-IN IS VITAL

o CHANGE MEASUREMENTS AS NECESSARY

IMPLEMENTING CHANGE

REWARD & RECOGNITION

KEY SUCCESS FACTORS

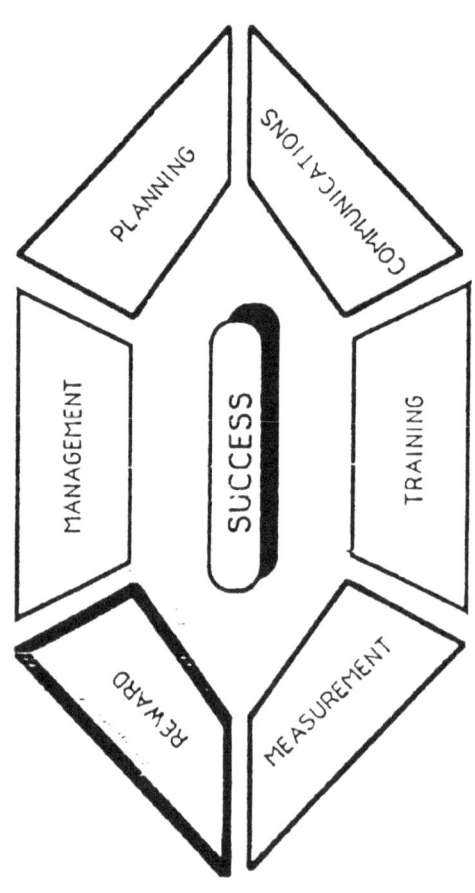

o   PROVIDE PROPER REWARD & RECOGNITION

o   RECOGNIZE INDIVIDUALS AND GROUPS

o   TIMELY MANNER

o   DISPLAY THE RESULTS OF SUCCESS

KEY SUCCESS FACTORS

IMPLEMENTING CHANGE

PLANNING
STRUCTURED PLAN
ALL LEVELS OF THE ORG.

COMMUNICATIONS
CLEARLY STATE GOALS
USE ALL AVAILABLE MEDIA

MANAGEMENT
INITIATION
PARTICIPATION

TRAINING
ALL PARTICIPANTS
SPECIFIC TASKS / DUTIES

REWARD
RECOGNIZE INDIVIDUAL &
GROUP PERFORMANCE
USE APPROPRIATE REWARDS

MEASUREMENT
ASSESS PERFORMANCE
INVOLVE EMPLOYEE

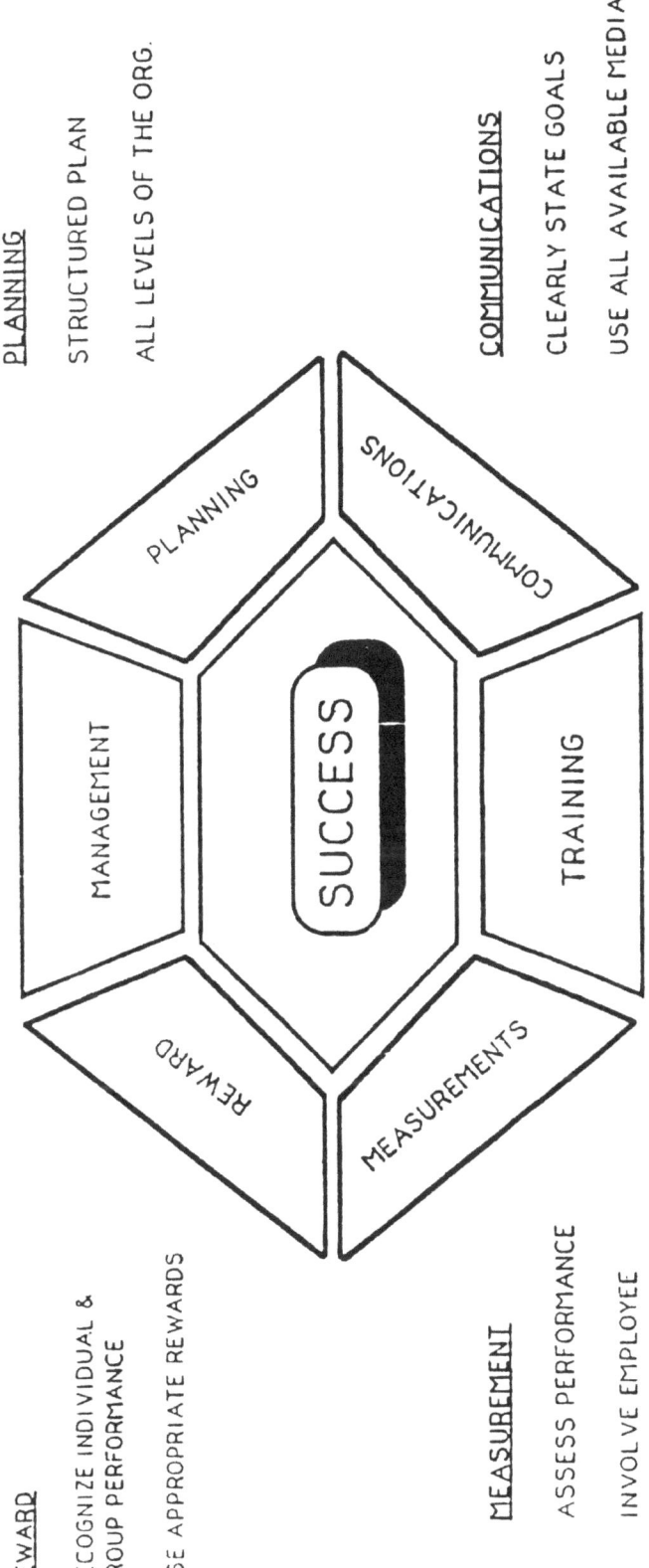

IMPLEMENTATION QUESTIONNAIRE

QUESTIONS	YES/NO	ACTIONS TO ASSURE SUCCESS
KEY SUCCESS FACTORS		
MANAGEMENT		
DO YOU HAVE APPROPRIATE SENIOR MANAGEMENT APPROVAL?		
IS SR. MGMT COMMITTED TO BE VISIBLE AND ACTIVELY PARTICIPATE?		
PLANNING		
HAS A STRUCTURED PLAN WHICH CONSIDERS ALL FACTORS BEEN DEVELOPED THAT INCLUDES SPECIFIC, ATTAINABLE, AND REALISTIC MILESTONES AND GOALS?		
HAS A REALISTIC SCHEDULE BEEN ESTABLISHED AND ACCEPTED BY THE PARTICIPANTS?		
COMMUNICATIONS		
HAVE YOU DEVELOPED A STRATEGY TO CLEARLY COMMUNICATE YOUR GOALS AND OBJECTIVES TO ALL LEVELS OF THE ORGANIZATION?		
HAVE TECHNIQUES FOR PROVIDING FEEDBACK BEEN DETERMINED?		
TRAINING		
HAS A TRAINING PLAN BEEN ESTABLISHED THAT WILL EDUCATE AND TRAIN ALL LEVELS OF THE ORGANIZATION?		
ARE THE APPROPRIATE RESOURCES AVAILABLE OR ATTAINABLE TO PROPERLY TRAIN THE PARTICIPANTS?		
MEASUREMENTS		
HAVE APPROPRIATE MEASUREMENTS BEEN DEVELOPED TO ASSESS PERFORMANCE TO STATED GOALS AND OBJECTIVES?		
ARE THEY CAPABLE OF BEING MODIFIED OR REPLACED WITH PROGRESS?		
REWARD AND RECOGNITION		
HAVE YOU ESTABLISHED A PROGRAM THAT WILL PROVIDE APPROPRIATE AND TIMELY RECOGNITION FOR THE PARTICIPANTS?		

IMPLEMENTATION QUESTIONNAIRE

QUESTIONS	YES/NO	ACTIONS TO ASSURE SUCCESS
WORK FORCE FACTORS		
INDIVIDUAL & GROUP CONSIDERATIONS		
HAS CONSIDERATION BEEN GIVEN FOR THE VALUES AND CONCERNS OF THE INDIVIDUAL WORKER?		
HAS CONSIDERATION BEEN TO GIVEN TO THE CHARACTERISTICS OF GROUP DYNAMICS?		
MANAGEMENT FACTORS		
LEADERSHIP		
IS SENIOR MANAGEMENT PREPARED TO MODIFY THEIR BEHAVIOR AND MANAGEMENT STYLE AS REQUIRED TO SUPPORT THIS INITIATIVE?		
ARE THEY WILLING TO SERVE AS MENTORS AND PROVIDE LEADERSHIP TO SUBORDINATES AS REQUIRED?		
ORGANIZATIONAL FACTORS		
STRUCTURE		
HAS CONSIDERATION BEEN GIVEN TO PREVIOUS ATTEMPTS TO CHANGE?		
WILL THE CURRENT STRUCTURE SUPPORT THE CHANGE PROCESS?		
PROCESS & PROCEDURES		
WILL CURRENT PROCESSES OR PROCEDURES HAVE TO BE MODIFIED?		
WILL ANY NEW ONES HAVE TO BE WRITTEN?		
COMMUNITY IMPACT		
WILL THIS CHANGE HAVE AN ADVERSE EFFECT ON THE LOCAL COMMUNITY?		
HAS THIS IMPACT BEEN ADDRESSED WITH THE APPROPRIATE CORPORATE AND CUMMUNITY LEADERS?		

IMPLEMENTATION QUESTIONNAIRE

QUESTIONS	YES/NO	ACTIONS TO ASSURE SUCCESS
UNDERLYING CONSIDERATIONS		
ENVIRONMENT HAS DUE CONSIDERATION BEEN GIVEN TO THE VALIDITY AND SOURCE OF THIS PROPOSED CHANGE?		
IS IT REQUIRED OR BEING DONE IN RESPONSE TO A CURRENT TREND?		
TECHNICAL HAVE THE TECHNOLOGICAL IMPACTS BEEN GIVEN ADEQUATE CONSIDERATION?		
WILL THIS CHANGE GIVE US A PREEMPTIVE CAPABILITY?		
POLITICAL HAVE YOU NEGOTIATED FOR THE PROPER RESOURCES?		
HAS A PLAN BEEN DEVELOPED TO OBTAIN THOSE RESOURCES THAT ARE IN SHORT SUPPLY?		
CULTURAL IS THE PREVAILING CORPORATE CULTURE AMENABLE TO CHANGE?		
HAVE THE AREAS OF RESISTANCE BEEN IDENTIFIED?		
RISK ARE THE NECESSARY RESOURCES BOTH HUMAN AND CAPITAL AVAILABLE?		
HAVE YOU IDENTIFIED WHO IS ACCOUNTABLE FOR THE VARIOUS TASKS?		
HAVE YOU ADDRESSED ANY GAPS THE PLAN MAY CONTAIN?		
ARE THE RESPONSIBLE PARTIES PREPARED TO NEGOTIATE AND COMPROMISE TO ATTAIN THE OVERALL OBJECTIVE?		

MAJOR INITIATIVE SURVEY   - SUMMARY -

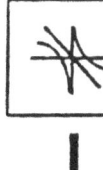

ENGINEERING
OPERATIONS
SUPPORT

- 19 OF 30 COMPANIES RESPONDED TO THE SURVEY

- RESPONSE SUMMARY:

	COMPLETED SURVEYS				NUMBER OF CHANGES (3 YEARS)		
	MATRIX(13)	NON-MATRIX(6)	TOTAL		MATRIX(6)	NON-MATRIX(4)	TOTAL
HIGHLY SUCCESSFUL	15	4	19		9	4	13
SOMEWHAT SUCCESSFUL	11	9	20		27	7	34
UNSUCCESSFUL	9	4	13		19	3	22
	35	17	52		55	14	69

- SOMEWHAT SUCCESSFUL RESPONSES WERE VIRTUALLY IDENTICAL TO THE HIGHLY SUCCESSFUL DATA THESE RESPONSES WERE CONSIDERED AS PART OF THE HIGHLY SUCCESSFUL SUMMARY

- THE TWO-BY-TWO GRID TECHNIQUE WAS USED TO CATEGORIZE AND DISPLAY THE RESPONSES

- THE CONCLUSIONS DRAWN FROM THE SURVEY RESPONSES INDICATE GENERAL TRENDS

- NO CORRELATION COULD BE MADE BETWEEN THE TYPE OF INITIATIVE AND IT'S SUCCESS

- INITIATIVES BEGUN MOST RECENTLY APPEAR TO BE MORE SUCCESSFUL

To reach the author:

email: rrokosz@gmail.com

Peak Performance Group

Books may be purchased at
www.Amazon.com

About the Author

Rick Rokosz is originally from Chicago IL. Rick has a bachelor's and a master's degree in Business from the Anderson College of Business at Regis University where he is currently a Term Professor facilitating graduate and undergraduate business courses. He has received numerous awards for excellence in teaching. He enjoyed a lengthy career in Aerospace and is a retired Lockheed Martin Corporation executive. His extensive background and real-world business experience makes him a highly sought-after speaker.

Rick is a Viet Nam Veteran having served in the U.S. Army as a non-commissioned officer in charge of field artillery operations in Da Nang, South Viet Nam. His military awards include the Bronze Star, and Viet Nam Presidential Unit Citation among several others. Rick contributes to the community as a certified SCORE Mentor specializing in the development and delivery of workshops to help individuals create new businesses. He also owns Peak Performance Group (a business training/consulting firm).

He is married, has two grown sons and three wonderful grandchildren. Rick and his wife reside in the beautiful Verde Valley of Cottonwood, Arizona. Rick published a work entitled Implementing Change: The Dynamics of the Change Process in the Aerospace Industry (1991) which is being reprinted, and he is currently working on a collection of leadership lessons about managing from the dark side called 'A Pirate's Manifesto'. Watch for its release!

www.ingramcontent.com/pod-product-compliance
Lightning Source LLC
Chambersburg PA
CBHW081014170526
45158CB00010B/3035